Professor Stephen FitzGerald AO is Australia's leading authority on relations with Asia. He heads the influential Asia–Australia Institute at the University of New South Wales, the country's foremost vehicle for 'second track diplomacy' in East Asia, and chairs the Institute's region-wide forums in Asia in which leading East Asians debate ideas for shaping the region's political future.

Australia's first Ambassador to the People's Republic of China at the age of 34, and fluent in Mandarin, he has also had overlapping careers: as a China scholar, writing a definitive study of Beijing's relations with Chinese overseas and heading the Department of Far Eastern History and the Contemporary China Centre at the Australian National University; and as a businessman, since 1978 running a consultancy for Australian companies in Asia, principally China.

As chair of two Commonwealth committees—on Asian studies and on immigration—he was principal author of the watershed National Strategy for Asian Studies which became the blueprint for a decade of government policy for schools and universities, and the 'FitzGerald Report' on immigration, the most cited authority on the balance of interests in a non-discriminatory policy and on community attitudes to multiculturalism. He is also the Australian co-chair of a Joint Policy Committee for economic cooperation between the Northern Territory and Indonesian governments.

As Australian representative to the Commission for A New Asia based in Kuala Lumpur, he is a signatory to the visionary blueprint for Asia's future written by that Commission.

Professor FitzGerald lives in Sydney, and spends about a third of his year working in Northeast and Southeast Asia.

IS AUSTRALIA
AN ASIAN
COUNTRY?

Can Australia survive in an East Asian future?

STEPHEN FITZGERALD

ALLEN & UNWIN

First published in 1997 by
Allen & Unwin
9 Atchison Street
St Leonards NSW 2065
Australia
Phone: (61 2) 9901 4088
Fax: (61 2) 9906 2218
E-mail: frontdesk@allen-unwin.com.au
URL: http://www.allen-unwin.com.au

National Library of Australia
Cataloguing-in-Publication entry:

FitzGerald, Stephen, 1938– .
  Is Australia an Asian country?: can Australia survive in
  an East Asian future?

  Includes index.
  ISBN 1 86448 401 2.

  1. Pluralism (Social sciences)—Australia. 2. Nationalism—
  Australia. 3. Australia—Relations—Asia. I. Tile.

327.9405

Set in 10/12 pt Trump Mediaeval by DOCUPRO, Sydney
Printed by Australian Print Group, Maryborough, Vic.

10 9 8 7 6 5 4 3

Contents

Preface and Acknowledgments

This book is an argument about Australia's future. It concerns the preparedness and capability of Australian elites to deal with Asia, in particular East Asia, and at the same time to nurture the humanist, pluralist and democratic traditions of our society in the face of the challenges we will meet from East Asia over the next 30 years.

There is much to be concerned about, and this has to do with the way in which Australian elites in general have responded to Asia, the aggregate performance which has brought us to where we are in late 1996. It is unfortunately the aggregate performance which counts, and where there have been problems it is in the aggregate that they show up. My argument is about these problems, in the conviction that we have to address them if we are to secure a future with East Asia which ensures the benefit and survival of our society. But in writing it I am very conscious of the debt we all owe to the many individual exceptions to the general performance, most of whom are not recorded elsewhere in this book but whose work must be acknowledged and highly valued. These are individuals whose contribution to Australian thinking about and attitudes to Asia has been intellectual, forward-thinking and effective. I am referring not just to a Gough Whitlam (who is recorded here) but to the many others who went with him on the pilgrimage to create a new and hopeful vision for our future with Asia, like the late Mick Young. Nor simply to those others who because of their public office may have a high profile—Malcolm Fraser for the decision to admit Vietnamese refugees, Gareth Evans as Foreign minister, Paul Keating after becoming prime minister. But to the many who do not have a public profile—diplomats, academics, journalists, soldiers, artists, writers, teachers, scientists, business people. They are responsible for that side of Australia which gives us a possible future in Asia like that suggested in the final chapter. They may not concede that the issues are as I see them, but in concern for these issues I am far from being alone.

The issues addressed in this book have been with us for some time, and I have therefore gone back to some of the history and to some of the expression of my argument at the time in order to capture a sense of the issues as they emerged, as an evolving problem, and as they relate to today and tomorrow. These earlier papers and speeches are noted below.

The definition of Asia can be confusing. Very often it depends on quite specific and limited context. I use it to mean Asia in the way it is most generally understood today to include the two geographical regions of East Asia (from Mongolia in the north to Indonesia in the south and, one hopes, also Australia, and west as far as Myanmar) and South Asia (comprising India and the surrounding countries, and west to include Afghanistan but not being too dogmatic about a western extremity). When using the word 'Asia' in relation to our education or intellectual and cultural horizons or business interests it is usually in reference to these two regions, and precise definition of where these begin and end is not important. 'Asia-literacy', for example, is intended to have this broad, inclusive meaning, allowing that people who are Asia-literate may be literate only in respect of one or more parts of this Asia.

For the more specific question of what 'Asia' Australia itself might be part of, relating to the political future of our society, the focus and the definition are limited to one of these geographical regions, East Asia (see Chapter 1, Endnote 1). The term 'Asia-Pacific', which I generally avoid, has policy and practical problems for Australia which are discussed in Chapter 1 and elsewhere.

As this book went to the publisher in late October 1996, a new Australian race debate burst around the ears of Australians, and into the pages of the Asian press and the consciousness of interested Asians. It is said to have been caused by an independent MP and to have something to do with a debate on immigration. This is wrong on both counts. The cause was not the statements of an inconsequential MP but a failure in leadership. There have been many individual racist outbursts of this kind, within the Parliament as outside it, and there always will be. But the ravings of an ignorant bigot on this occasion could have been swept aside by immediate and unambiguous statements by the Prime Minister and his Cabinet team. That is leadership.

An immigration debate would of course be welcome, as would debate on multiculturalism. But this debate is not about the serious matters of immigration, or even the serious matter of multiculturalism. It is about racism. And it is hardly debate. And 'leadership' in this 'debate' was abandoned to someone who had thought so little about the issue that even the facts were swept ignorantly aside. There is *always* unease about immigration, and there has been unease about multiculturalism ever since it was introduced. The Hawke Government bears some responsibility for what is happening now, having been warned in 1988 that the public felt excluded from decisions on immigration and multiculturalism and that public attitudes to multiculturalism were so negative that they would ultimately erode support for immigration, and having refused to take a lead and open a reasoned, informed and productive debate.

A part of the Australian media is also responsible, having behaved without ethical propriety or restraint in this matter, as it has done so often in the past in other matters which seriously affect our relations with Asia. With an indecent frenzy worthy of CNN with a good shooting war in prospect, some of them have rushed hither and thither to give extraordinary coverage to someone whose ignorance does not warrant more than passing notice and whose bigotry, deserving to remain in the dark, if built further into the heroic proportions it has been given, will destroy the great harmony, openness and tolerance of Australian society. These individuals in the media may protest that they are liberal. Collectively, many of them abandoned the responsibility of the freedom and independence our society accords them in a most illiberal pack hunt for ever more extreme and divisive outpourings. Asian opinion leaders will note this fact in the current fracas.

Australia is at a fork in the road to its future with Asia. One way is hard but promising and potentially immensely fulfilling. But Australia at the end of 1996 took some steps down the alternative way, which, if persisted in, as this book argues, could result in the extinction of some distinguishing features of this liberal, democratic and humanist society.

This book draws in part on previous occasional papers and speeches given in the last few years, considerably rewritten, updated and extended to reflect the evolution and growing seriousness of the issues addressed in its central argument. This is presented in the context of the situation Australia faces today and over the next 30 years, the writing for which is new. Chapter 2 is partly drawn from *Australia's China*, the Fiftieth George Ernest Morrison Lecture in Ethnology 1989, published by the Australian National University; Chapter 3 presents material from the Asia Leaders' Forum at Bali in September 1994, which is used without direct ascription, and an address at the Asia Leaders' Forum on APEC in 1993. Chapter 5 is based on the 1990 Buntine Oration at the Australian College of Education, for whose material, and for some of Chapter 6, I acknowledge a great debt to the contribution of Jim Wilson, former director of the Asia–Australia Institute. Chapter 7 draws on an address given at the RIPAA National Conference in November 1993. Chapter 8 is substantially drawn from the published 1993 Annual Lecture to the St James Ethics Centre. The Hong Kong material in Chapter 9 draws on an address given to the University of Hong Kong in November 1994.

Beyond these specific debts, the ideas in this book have a lineage which belongs to other people. These are people into the orbit of whose intellectual influence I have chanced, and who pushed or inspired the intellectual development that brings me to take up the argument presented in the chapters which follow. There was a rough sequence to my exposure to their influence, which began with George Wilson, who not only taught me Asian history but taught that it matters. And thereafter, Julian Wu, who taught that learning Chinese is not just about language; Jack Harris, whose life exemplifies continuous, lifelong expansion of the intellect (and who taught how to enjoy the Asia we learnt about—and sometimes lent me the money to continue both); Greg Clark, who showed that commitment of Asia knowledge to Australia's political development could be thankless but was fundamental; Gough Whitlam, whose combination of intellect and vision was inspiring and compelling; Mick Young, who taught me that there were many Australias I did not know; Wang Gungwu, that best of scholars, who shows how to intellectualise knowledge in historical depth, political breadth and social responsibility; David Block, relentless in making one intellectualise the issue; and the experience at the Asia–Australia Institute which, beginning in October 1990, found and pushed my 'pilgrim soul'.

It was my wife, Helen (Gay), who actually taught me how to think in the first place.

John Iremonger, publisher, asked Venetia Somerset, editor and writer, to see if she could worry this book into existence (over a few short months in which I was to be mainly in planes and hotel rooms in Asia, from Beijing to Brunei). The ideas and scattered pieces already written would still be where they were then without her critical role in setting up the 'architecture' which facilitated and forced the writing. I am in her debt, and can think of no better way to thank her than by commending her warmly to any other author in a similar situation.

My colleagues, at the Asia–Australia Institute but particularly in Stephen FitzGerald & Co., have often had to endure my distraction with things which take me away from what I am meant to be doing with them for 'core business'. They do so with more good-humoured resignation than I deserve, and none more so than Clare Starr, most valued colleague, and Virgo, who does all the worrying, for me and for everyone else. My colleagues Tang Luhua, Emma Cole, Linda Burke and Michael Wesley helped calmly in the last-minute rush to locate, update or tidy up references and citations, for which I gratefully offer much thanks.

Abbreviations

AAI	Asia–Australia Institute
AGPS	Australian Government Publishing Service
AIDAB	Australian International Development Assistance Bureau
ANU	Australian National University
APEC	Asia-Pacific Economic Cooperation
ARF	ASEAN Regional Forum
ASAA	Asian Studies Association of Australia
ASEAN	Association of South-East Asian Nations
ASEM	ASEAN–Europe Meeting
AUSAID	Australian Agency for International Development
COAG	Council of Australian Governments
C-SCAP	Council on Security Cooperation in the Asia-Pacific
DFAT	Department of Foreign Affairs and Trade
DIFF	Development Import Finance Facility
EAEC	East Asian Economic Caucus
EFTA	European Free Trade Association
PRC	People's Republic of China
SBS	Special Broadcasting Service
SEATO	South-East Asia Treaty Organisation

CHAPTER 1

Do we belong in Asia?

In March 1996 a meeting took place in Bangkok. Australia did not much remark it at the time, but it was a remarkable event. 'Europe', in the form of the European Union, had come to sit down with 'Asia', in the form of a coalition of states from East Asia. Multilateral in form but bilateral in essence, it was the first meeting of its kind in the history of contact between these two parts of the world. They met as equals, although if there was suitor on either side it was on the European rather than the Asian. Four hundred years of unfortunate history at an end, without hurrah. It closed a door on this past. But it was more a portent of the future, of the next hundred years and beyond.

This was the meeting known as ASEM, the ASEAN–Europe Meeting. In political coalition initially just for the purpose of this meeting with Europe, the Asian participants were nevertheless conscious that this was both precedent and definition. They were at the beginning of the definition of a region, and a future for that region. There was therefore disagreement, and argument, and lobbying and brokering over who would attend and who would not. The question at the back of it all was not just who would speak for 'Asia' at this meeting but which group of states could be said to constitute an 'Asia', hitherto non-existent in such form. And because agreement on a definition was difficult, it came down to definition by exclusion. But it was a definition. While it was not quite the division of the world George Orwell imagined in *1984*, when the world looks back on 1996 from 2026 this will probably be seen as the point at which the definition of an 'Asian Community' really began.[1]

Australia was not present at this meeting, on either side. It was not 'Europe'. It sued for inclusion as 'Asia'. It was vetoed by Malaysia. But just as significant as the Malaysian veto was that the other East Asian states were not prepared to risk their consensus for Australia's benefit, and went along with the exclusion. And by that collective decision, the group of states which had come together in coalition ostensibly just for an economic summit had made a definition of this Asia which was political, and cultural, and in some measure also racial.

While Australia may yet be admitted to this coalition, the message is one of utmost gravity for this country. Europe was not an option for it. Asia was not open to it. That part of the world which is completely dominant in Australia's economic, immigration, tourism and education flows, and in political and cultural influence in Australia's regional habitat, was closed to Australia politically. An outsider, Australia had no vote in this coalition, no voice. It was not part of the 'ingroup'—an ominous exclusion in the cultural imperatives of East Asian societies. And here is the central argument of this book. To be denied participation in the critical political councils of the coalition of states which dominates us economically is comparable to a colonial status for Australia. Threatening to Australia's capacity to determine its own future in the short term, it will, if it persists into the longer term, diminish our independence and extinguish some defining features of Australian society.

How can this have happened? How can Australia not have foreseen such an event? How can we have missed the signals of an emerging East Asia until it was almost, possibly still is, too late?

There is no single explanation, but there is an overriding one. The Australian commitment to Asia was not one of the mind. It was not informed by deep knowledge. It was not thought out or conceptualised within an understanding of the elemental forces at work within Asian societies. It was in this sense not an intellectual engagement; it was not intellectualised. It was therefore almost incapable of sensitivity to subtlety or sub-text or silence, or even to direct and open alternative Asian views of this region and its future.

This failing was a failing of government, but it was a failing across the total spectrum of Australian elites. There were individual exceptions, but in the totality, in the aggregate of perceptions and attitudes, it was true of the Labor Government and also of the Coalition which is now in government, and of their advisers, and of the senior levels of all government agencies. It was true of the ruling elites in business and in the universities, and also in the media. While the failure to win a place in a more tightly defined Asia ought to have been alarming, therefore, it should not have been surprising.

The irony is that many Australians should have thought otherwise. Australia had actually recently embraced Asia, or at least an idea of Asia. This had taken some time. Australian foreign policy had of course been built originally, at the time of Federation, on an exclusion of its own, which kept it apart from Asia in human and political terms. Even under the great 1950s and 1960s Colombo Plan, Asians could come to study but could not stay. There may be both conscious and unconscious pay-back in the Malaysian exclusion of Australia now from its definitions of what is Asian!

The great postwar symbol of Australia's attitude to Asia was its joining hands with America in the policy of non-recognition and containment of China. But the watershed decision by the Whitlam Government in 1972 to recognise China did not secure the embrace of Asia. After Whitlam and for the next twenty years there was agonising and temporising, with rushes of enthusiasm and advance, followed by dismay and retreat when Asian societies did not behave as Australians expected them to, politically or economically. There was much verbal backtracking: 'No, not me mate. I never said we were part of Asia. No, we don't actually belong to Asia. We're not an Asian *people*. No, no, we're not *Asian*'. Government was often emotional rather than visionary and rational, as Whitlam had been, particularly in relation to China. The Coalition often could not make up its mind, for example on Asian immigration. Business was alternately flushed with excitement—now China, now Thailand, now Indonesia, now Vietnam, now China again—or bathed in cynicism, the latter often concealing an inability to grapple intellectually or commercially with what it found in Asian countries. The universities discovered Asia with the cash register, but when the till did not immediately fill, 'wise' heads in chancelleries around Australia were expounding the more serious opportunities in North America and Europe! Private schools of English emerged to feed on Asian students like blowflies in a hot Australian summer, and disappeared, leaving the government to clean up the mess. There was no national consensus about an Australian future in Asia.

But elite opinion came together unexpectedly some time around the turn of the decade, at the very beginning of the 1990s. Almost suddenly, resistance seemed to fold and all the major political parties and all significant interest groups seemed to be in unison on the central importance of the region to Australia's future. There is no single event to which this change can be attached, but it was first apparent some time after Keating became prime minister and by the general election in March 1993, it was there. It was not remotely an issue in that election, from any quarter.

But what Australians imagined this Asia to be, and hence also what they imagined to be the nature of the Australian future with Asia, had not much to do with how Asian societies actually were or how they saw themselves in this future. Even at the time of this conversion, therefore, Australia had still not been educated for Asia. It did not intellectualise the experience or the expectation. There was no over-the-horizon perspective. And there is still no contemplation of what it might mean for Australian society in 30 years' time or whether the end point will be good for us, or bad.

The Asian challenge for Australia is not economic or commercial. It is intellectual, and the issues are political and cultural. In the second half of 1996, leading politicians and business people were reported as saying that minor political matters had got in the way of an essentially economic relationship with China. They were not alone in that. Senior Australian officials spoke in similar terms. The political matters on this occasion had to do with Taiwan (Australian ministerial visits and proposed uranium sales), Tibet (an impending visit to Australia by the Dalai Lama), and above all perceived Australian complicity in what China sees as a new US policy of containment of China. These are not minor matters for China and they are highly political. But the analysis illustrates the intellectual problem for Australia. It is not that we have to agree with China on these issues. Far from it! But to see our relations with China as 'economic' and these other, political matters as simply getting in the way is, nationally, so far from reality and informed analysis as to raise a question of whether we are capable of looking after our country. These are big issues for China because they are political for China. They are fundamental for China, and they will not go away. Only five months earlier, in the Taiwan Straits crisis of March 1996, the Chinese Government had shown it was willing to put economic and other interests at stake in the pursuit of political goals. Human behaviour, on economic and other matters, is driven by human and political considerations which have their roots in history and culture. This is true of China, as it is of Malaysia, or Indonesia, or Japan, or Australia. The economic and commercial matters are important, and often pre-eminent, and they are hard. But they are part of a bigger and harder picture.

So the question of how we make our future with Asia, or whether we have a future, depends on how well we can apply our minds. It doesn't mean we just have to get the economic relations right, or even the regional security. And it doesn't mean we have to become Asian, a popular windmill for tilting at by people who can't face the intellectual challenge. It means we have to intellectualise our engagement, in relation to three fundamental matters. One is what has happened to change Asia. One is our own circumstances in relation to Asia, including in respect to other parts of the world and particularly the United States. And one is the future of this region over the very long term and how we fit into that and how it will affect us.

That future will not be one in which the United States, or any other power with which we have shared cultural heritage or political philosophies or processes or institutions, is the determining force in the part of the world in which we live. The dominant political force and cultural influence will be something like the coalition of East Asian states which emerged for ASEM, in turn under the pervasive and dominant influence of China. This will be an utterly new experience for Australia, and there will be no certainty that we will be able to handle it in a way which protects fundamental features of our society which make it attractive to us, and to the hundreds of thousands of people from other countries who seek to settle here. There is a question mark over how we will fare and how far our political and social system will be able to survive the experience.

ASEM is not the end of the line. It could be the beginning of the end of the line, but I think not. I hope not. But even if it was only a close brush with destiny, its intimation of a possibly less than fortunate future for Australia must never be forgotten, and for that reason I have taken it as a leitmotif for this book. It is not of course the ASEM meeting as such, but

ASEM as a shorthand for a closed coalition of East Asian states which began in 1996 and which excluded Australia.

We like to think our society has changed, and part of this book is concerned with defending our record of change against the critics in Asia who say we have stood still. But the magnitude of change in Asian societies—political and cultural and not simply economic—has been breathtaking by comparison. And while we seem to perceive its importance in some respects, we do not seem to apprehend its political import, for them or for us.

Some time ago I talked with the retired long-serving Prime Minister of Singapore, Lee Kuan Yew. I wanted him to come here to stir the Australian possum about Asia. He said: 'I don't know about that. If I'm approached by Japanese who want to hang something on what they know I'll say I accept because the Japanese will listen, and try to do something about change. I've been to Australia. I've talked bluntly about Australia and Asia. But I see no change. No one takes any notice. I also look at where Singapore was in 1965 and where Australia was, and where we both are now. We had nothing then but our hands and our brains. We have had to work, and be resilient, and change. Australia seems not to want to change.'

Lee's bleak view of Australia was unjustifiable on many counts, and in what he had to say elsewhere in that meeting about our alleged racism he was anachronistic. But he spoke a truth about an Asian perception of Australia, and in some measure also about the reality.

He spoke a greater truth about change in Asia. Over roughly 30 years, Japan has moved from 'those Nips we beat the shit out of in the war' to become the centre of world financial power, buying up the great symbols of America (the Rockefeller Centre, Columbia Pictures), and even those of Australia (the local abattoirs, and perhaps the tomato sauce factory). Japan has become our major trading partner, a major foreign investor, and a major source of tourist income. It is spending to the consti-tutional limit on defence. It is the world's largest giver of aid and is being pushed by the United States and some in Asia to take an active political and leadership role in Asia, 'our' part of the world.

Over the same period, Singapore's standard of living has surpassed New Zealand's and Australia's. Indonesia, Malaysia, Thailand and even China have been achieving annual growth rates of 8 per cent and above. Taiwan, patronised as a political supplicant when I first went to work in Canberra in 1961, has reserves of around US$85 billion, almost ten times the reserves of Australia and about half the size of Australia's net foreign debt. The size of the Indonesian middle class has passed the total population of Australia. South Korea, once regarded in Australia as a corrupt and insular little country, is a net aid donor, which gave bountifully to the newly free states of Eastern Europe when we could not. South Korea! To which we, having succoured them with arms in the 1950s, now go begging for alms in the 1990s to assist in the education of our children!

Over this period, the great wars of Asia (Vietnam, the Asian theatre of the Cold War) have come to an end, and the great process of cultural rediscovery and escape from poverty has taken off. The Asia of Somerset Maugham, which was the kind of filter through which Australians viewed Asia, has been peeled away. And what we have is a cosmopolitan jostling of countries and cultures and peoples more distinct one from another than anything in Europe, but all of them buoyed on a current of mutual discovery, which is bearing them inexorably towards a new kind of region, in which Asia is both a collection of states and a Community.

This is partly where our intellectual problem begins: making simplicities where intellectual effort would see nothing but complexities.

We began with 'Asiatics' in the nineteenth century and this persisted well into the last decades of the twentieth century. We are all given to stereotypes, and that is also how I began my own engagement with Asia. Walking with Eric Walsh (later a well-known journalist and political and business figure, *bon vivant* and restaurateur) in Dixon Street in Sydney's Chinatown, some 30 years ago, with my newly acquired Chinese language (Mandarin), and in search of a bottle of Rose Dew liquor, I was elbowed in the ribs and urged to ask for the wine in Chinese. In an urban version of a Chinese trade store up the Sepik River or somewhere in Western Sumatra, I spoke to the Chinese behind the counter, a tiny, wizened woman with a nut-brown face and cataract-clouded eyes, who would have been on the high side of 90 years old. She listened, uncomprehending. I asked again, certain by now that she was Cantonese and did not speak Mandarin. She screwed up her face, looked up at me and said, 'Don't yer speak Austrailyan?'

This story illustrates something of the mental stereotypes

we have in thinking about Asia. I had assumed, and I suppose Walsh had also, something from this woman's physiognomy which was entirely unjustified. Australia began its long coming to terms with Asia with similar assumptions and stereotyping. There was of course no such thing as Asia, and there was not such a people as the Asian people. The word was a European invention. Before the Europeans there was no such word in any of the languages of the region. They came to use it to refer to a part of the world which was clearly not Europe or Africa or the Americas. But it meant nothing. Even where it begins or ends is still not agreed. Within the Asian Studies Association of Australia, the body which brings together the professional Asianists, there is some tension over the western extremity of this enormous region: how far does it extend into the Arab world, and does that take it all the way through North Africa to the Atlantic Ocean? When I was inquiring into our immigration policies for the Australian government in 1987–88, I discovered that the government worked on a definition of Asia which begins at the Bosporus and goes all the way to somewhere in the mid-Pacific Ocean.

So in the sense of defining a boundary, in ethnic, cultural, linguistic, religious, philosophical, political, economic or geographic terms, 'Asia' in its original definition didn't have too much meaning. And that's why we get other terms such as 'the Asia-Pacific region', which does not have much meaning either on any of the terms above, except to define an economic relationship (but not an economic region). APEC (the Asia Pacific Economic Cooperation forum) is Asian only in the sense that it joins North and South America with East Asia. Asia may include Australia. Asia is not the United States.

But the term Asia-Pacific was taken up more enthusiastically in Australia than in any other country, partly to simplify what was complex and challenging, and partly for another reason which I will come to shortly. The term took on almost comical connotations. Australians spoke of Asia-Pacific when they meant only Asia, and of learning Asia-Pacific languages when they meant only Chinese, Japanese and Indonesian, and Asia-Pacific growth rates when they meant only those in East Asia. It was a double distortion, because it not only failed to disaggregate Asia into its component societies but also aggregated it into something which encompassed North America and parts of South America. It also contributed to the problem which subsequently emerged for Australia in ASEM. For there was a third distortion, in that in one part of Asia, East Asia, there was beginning to emerge something which really was an Asia region in more than European nomenclature, but which was obscured for us by our preoccupation with APEC.

There was something else which Australia tended to assume about Asia, and that was that we would necessarily find acceptance there. This was always open to question. In one sense, geography, we may be logically a part of East Asia. The word 'austral' means 'south', and the Australian continent is the centrepiece of what Magellan named 'Austral Asia', southern Asia. To Europeans, there was 'Asia', and there were various parts of it, and this continent by that European geographical definition was simply part. In his last year as Australian Foreign minister, Gareth Evans, seized with the urgency of identifying Australia with what was happening in East Asia independently of APEC, took up this idea with his introduction of the term 'East Asian hemisphere', which was a geographical, or cartographical, way of defining Australia in.[2]

But cartography is unfortunately not enough, and this raises the second issue to which we have to apply our intellects. At a time when Australians began to think of themselves as part of Asia, or at least as having a future in Asia, I know of few East Asians who say with no reservation at all that Australia belongs to their region, however they define it. They may like individual Australians, and some who have been here may even like Australia. But they don't regard it as being a part of what they are. This is not only a matter of perceived ethnic or cultural difference. There are enough differences of that kind between the countries of the region to make it a fact of life in all their dealings with each other. But Southeast Asians, for example, who may not like Japan, nevertheless tend to concede that Japan is part of the region. But not necessarily Australia. Many countries around the region have attitudes which sit uncomfortably with their neighbours. China, for example, has cultural arrogance, but few in the region question that China belongs there. In Australia's case, the fundamental problem is that while we may have come to mouth the sentiment of belonging to the region, we have done too little to belong in human terms or to make the necessary cultural and intellectual adjustment. And that is unforgivable, and for as long as we continue in this mode we will always be outsiders, however much we may participate in the formal institutions of the region.

Australians have to bear two things in mind about their

circumstances in Asia. One is that Australia has no natural or historical friends there. With Britain we had the strongest of familial ties, buttressed by common institutions and common ideas. These included ideas about the state and the role of the individual in relation to the state. These were the ties that underpinned our economic and political relationships and also locked us into the international politics of Europe and North America. We were one of them. We have no such ties with any of the Asian countries. So when we go into these countries we must go realising that we are there not as of right, that we can't assume acceptance, that we are still a guest and not part of the family. The other has to do with belonging, and how one moves from being a guest, welcome or unwelcome, into a more intimate and accepting relationship as part of the group. What kept our relationship with Britain strong was that we grew up with a knowledge of things British—our fairy tales, our nursery rhymes, our stories. A child growing up in Hobart would have been more familiar with the streets and districts of London than of Sydney.

We do not have these threads of interrelatedness with any society in Asia, and we have done almost nothing to develop them. Our universities, for example, failed almost totally to cultivate their Asian alumni, until financial imperatives drove them to do it in the late 1980s. We have been lazy about Asia to the point of irresponsibility. It is now 30 years since Donald Horne coined the phrase 'the lucky country' to describe both the bountiful largesse of Australia's natural resources and the prodigal excess of its people, as they lay on the beaches and around the barbecues imbibing the good life, and not caring too much about productivity, restructuring for the future, or international competitiveness.

In the build-up to the lucky election in 1993 which dusted them back into power, Australian Labor ministers, seeking to turn complacency into competition and appeal to Australians to exalt and utilise the things of the mind rather than the yachting races and quick-rich business sleaze which had so diverted the Labor leadership in the preceding decade, turned to an awkward hortatory slogan, 'the clever country' (the words 'intelligent' or 'excellent' being presumably too uncomfortable). I doubt whether most Australians even then had the interest to turn what was once the lucky country into a clever country. That may well become possible in the future. But it depends on how Australia balances two characteristics of Australian society, the 'lazy country' and the 'lovely country'. The latter is a reality which is touched on throughout this book, and in its ideal form in the final chapter.

But first we have to deal with 'the lazy country'. This is an outgrowth of the lucky country and is the negative aspect of the laid-back, tolerant, accepting Australian. It is not really the fault of the average Australian. It is probably mostly the fault of Australian leadership. For years laziness was encouraged through indulgent social welfare policies, policy and legislative concessions to shorter working hours and increased benefits for no productivity gains and, critically, increased wages with no concomitant increase in skills. In Australia you get paid to go on holiday, and you are paid an additional 17.5 per cent loading on your wage while you are on holiday. Government, unions, business and universities were all culpable in one way or another. Governments did not educate the people about the costs of this self-indulgence, and they were lackadaisical about the need to cultivate intellect and skill for tomorrow.

Beginning in the 1980s with the Hawke Government and the Keating reforms, and then with everyone at the top end of Australian life, Australia hurried to overcome these problems, with admirable urgency but predictably slow results. It's extremely hard to turn around a national psyche, when in the past people had been led by all the elites in the country to expect that they didn't have to exert themelves. The whole country had been allowed, encouraged, to slow down. Let someone else do the work. Let someone else worry. Let someone else be 'clever'. One of the most telling Australian statistics is that as we entered the 1990s about 12 per cent of the Australian workforce of English-speaking origin was illiterate, and that figure was roughly double what it was in the mid-1980s; in some trades the figure was around 40 per cent. In a country where school education has been free and compulsory for nearly a century!

Although the importance of Asia has now passed into the vocabulary of Australia, there is almost no evidence that private or public sector Australia sees any real link between a need to actually do anything about the skills of its own *mainstream* employees and what it now says Australia ought to be doing in or with Asia. You can search among the Australian head-hunters and newspaper ads almost in vain to find anyone seeking, in a senior, mainstream executive position, skills, experience or connections that relate specifically to Asia.

The case for Asia skills and expertise, and the radical reorientation of education, can be argued on the grounds of intellectual and cultural imperatives alone, wherever one is in the world. What the geographical proximity of Asia to Australia does is simply to add immediacy and urgency to our need to do something about it. And the fact that we have been so late in coming to it is why our looming problems with the new Asia are at base intellectual and cultural.

What do we think and say of Japanese, for example, or Chinese who come to Australia on official or commercial business and who speak no foreign language? Australians often laugh. But look at the preparedness of Australian elites, the products of Australian education. In the whole of the Australian Parliament there is still only one person who is fluent in an Asian language. There has never been a permanent head of the Australian foreign service fluent in an Asian language, or, for that matter, of any other Australian government department. The same goes for the vice-chancellors of all the Australian universities, the general editors of our major newspapers and magazines and heads of television stations, the general staff of the defence forces, and the heads of our major and most of our minor corporations. I first wrote these few sentences in 1988, in *A National Strategy for the Study of Asia in Australia*,[3] but there is barely need to alter one word in 1996, and the list goes on. Why? Because it's not regarded as important, because the acquisition of Asian languages is too much trouble, because we're doing all right in Asia anyway, or so it's believed. In many institutions there is still a philosophy which actually makes a virtue of the lack of linguistic skills.

If we add to the language issue the fact that all but a sprinkling of these same Australian elites has never had any general education in or about Asia, we begin to see the problem. And because in any democratic society there has to be some broad comprehension of major national policies and goals, the breathtaking absence of Asia from the general education and training of the populace creates a monumental knowledge and comprehension gap between the electorate and the leadership's policies to involve Australia more intimately with Asia.

Business elites have been no better. For many years now, most of our trade has been with Asia; Asia is a major source of our foreign investment, a substantial factor in our tourist industry, and an important source of our immigrants. This makes all the more astonishing the way most Australians still go about trying to do business in Asia. Without any natural linguistic and cultural advantages, they do almost none of the things they would do by way of preparation in Australia. They will send someone to do business in Asia who not only has no language or other Asia-related skills but who has never before been outside Australia (and who is still sometimes even asked to be the 'Asia representative', covering a territory from India to Japan). They will ignore the role of government or the military in an Asian country until it is too late.

This ought to require the application of a great deal of education and skilling. Yet until the last few years, the nation had done nothing even about the skilling of the teaching force which will be training the people who will have to handle Australia and its relations with Asia over the next twenty to thirty years.

This book is about that 30-year future with Asia and what could be made of it and how. There is also some recent and contemporary history. Without the history we will not be able to make much sense of the future.

The starting-point, for both the history and the future, is: what happened at the turn of the decade to bring Australian elites into near unanimous recognition that Asia was our future, and yet which did not enable us to gain admission to the first conclave of the company of states which will probably make up an East Asian Community and, one way or another, decisively determine Australia's future?

There will be as many explanations as there are Australian politicians claiming to have been the one to have discovered Asia. But in my view the explanation is that what happened was a change of heart, a commitment of the pocket, but intellectual only in so far as faith is rationalised into belief. The heart and the pocket, but not the mind.

There was one other contributing factor which was fundamentally important. Being mixed up with Asia was very confronting for a country which had so recently been abandoned by Britain and was in the process of loosening ties with the United States. So there was much agnosticism about Asia. Notwithstanding Whitlam's great vision, the period from 1972 to 1990 was one of continuing uncertainty, disagreement, false starts, and hesitation at total commitment. What enabled this to turn into belief was, I think, APEC, but for APEC reasons, not Asia reasons. Because APEC provided a comfort, an escape into the idea that the world had not changed, need not change. Because in APEC Australia had the company of the still dominant power, the United States, with Canada and New Zealand as a bonus. The white man's club.

I am not suggesting that this was conscious on the part of the Australian Government, and it would be wrong and deeply offensive to the liberal convictions of many of my friends in government at the time to suggest that it was what they had in mind. But it certainly opened the way for the consensus, the embrace of 'Asia' as we saw it in the early 1990s. We had Asia-Pacific, not Asia. For Asia-Pacific you might not have to change at all.

So Asia-Pacific, and APEC, became a substitute for Asia. It was what I have called a Clayton's Asia. There were many who thought that APEC would deliver us Asia and us to Asia, under the secure umbrella of the dominant cultures of the dominant power in APEC—America.

One of the big problems we face is how to get rid of this orientation, which is clearly very real in the Coalition, much more so than it was in Labor. Because it is not simply misguided. It is fatally distracting and misleading. Gareth Evans was originally irritated by this interpretation of our participation in APEC. He took issue, and used to ask me why I was 'anti-APEC'. I was not anti-APEC, at least not on the objectives it had for all our countries of keeping the American economy open, and engaged with Asian economies. But APEC, elevated as it was by Australia to the main event in multilateral regional arrangements, was for some a welcome relief, for some an excuse, but for all a distraction from the really hard task. This task involves, while maintaining the integrity of our own political and social system, coming to terms intellectually with Asia and Asians. Not on American or 'Western' ground, but on our ground and on Asians' ground. On their terms, taking account of their cultural and historical backgrounds. In their languages. With their politics and political imperatives. And their sensitivities, and their perceptions of Australia. And their ideas and initiatives for multilateral regional cooperation. And the great global shift in the balance of power and influence in their favour. The world has changed forever. It no longer belongs to the European or the North American. And we are alone, exposed. Nowhere to go but Asia. APEC is not going to be the main event. Gareth Evans saw it, but he was under too much constraint. Keating began to see it also. But in the event they were swept from office in March 1996 and the new government would have us turn the clock back.

So the change in Australia, as many intelligent Asians perceived, has been incomplete. It was not necessarily racist as some Asians suggested, but it lacked a sense of how to make equality with Asians a real thing. It lacked humility. It lacked a sense that Asians could take the lead. It lacked sensitivity to what Asians said, or what they meant by what they said, or half said, or didn't say at all. Had we been intellectually trained and engaged, we might have made different decisions even if we still felt unequal and uncomfortable. Asian states which feel very unequal and uncomfortable with each other are making decisions about collaboration every day.

Australia not only did not hear or understand the alternative Asian voice. It opposed, attempted to thwart, and even mocked the few in East Asia who were talking openly about what some East Asians felt they had in common and about regional possibilities other than APEC. This was widespread in Canberra, among politicians and advisers and in the Department of Foreign Affairs and Trade. Asian ambassadors in Canberra spoke of it with concern, which they duly reported to their governments. And Australia—government, official, and in much of business and the universities—had no idea.

And so in March 1996, a meeting took place in Bangkok. Australia was excluded, not just by Malaysian veto but by the collective decision of the East Asians present. Imagine the momentous impact such an exclusion would have on Australian society in the year 2020. Or even in 2000.

CHAPTER 2

China as touchstone

What was it about Asia that Australia so lacked? One thing was the history—or a sense of the history—of Asian societies, of the historical experience of the region in general, of the deep long-term currents that bring about change and historical shift. To have that sense, however, requires considerable knowledge and a sustained interest in the history, and in how that has made contemporary society what it is and wants to be. Ironically, in the early period after World War II there were times when Australia understood the history and read the future better than other Westerners. Indonesian independence and Australian support for it and the extraordinary role of diplomat Tom Critchley is the best-known case, and there were others along the way. But by the time of the 1980s and 1990s, the increasing and at times single-minded obsession with contemporary economic competitiveness swept history aside and with it much of the capacity to judge, to be sensitive to things, including how human beings in Asia thought and felt, and why.

China was something of a touchstone in this particular Australian progression from the 1940s to the 1990s. And therefore, before we come to the future, it is worth going back to the history of our own society in relation to China, so that we might at least have a sense that there is a history.

The great C. P. FitzGerald, to whom I am not related but

would be pleased if I were, while condemned by Australian governments in the 1950s and 60s as a Red, and denied a visa to the United States, was not a Red. Far from it. He often protested that on many matters he was a political conservative. This makes him an interesting case in the politics of the time. It may also have been that Gang of Four China thought him a political conservative too, because despite repeated attempts I was not permitted to invite him to China as my personal guest for all the time I was ambassador in China.

I don't really care what Gang of Four China thought, but I do care what Patrick FitzGerald thought. Sinologist, historian and humanist, and founding Professor of Far Eastern History at the Australian National University, he was probably more identified with China in the public mind than anyone else in Australia in the 1950s and 60s. And much of his life, from 1950 onward, was very much about Australians and China and what this meant for our culture and identity. He was concerned with his own identity in relation to China and to his adopted Australia, and with the Australian identity. The challenge of Patrick FitzGerald in the 1950s was at base a challenge to Australians to come to their senses and consider who they were and where they were and how they should express that, and the touchstone was China.

In the mid-1980s the Australian Government was given to saying in various ways that China was the centre of our foreign policy, something that has since been denied by some officials. I was present on one occasion when Bob Hawke said it in a speech in Beijing. He was right in a way, even though he was meaning something different when he said it. China has been central for Australia in another, deeper sense in *domestic* Australian politics, and it has been so for a very long time.

A MEASURE OF AUSTRALIAN IDENTITY

If you take the left/right, communist/anti-communist dichotomies of the 1950s as being about what kind of society we wanted for Australia, the symbolism of China, disembodied China about which we knew nothing, was quintessentially about the Australian identity. In Australia, much more than in Britain, Europe or North America, it was China rather more than the Soviet Union which was invoked for this purpose. And it was an invocation from a deep-rooted tradition. Through the goldfields from which Chinese people were hounded, to the sugar-cane fields which they, not white Australians, pioneered and from which they were also driven by persecutory Queensland legislation, China, or Chinese, became a principal justification for White Australia. And White Australia was about preserving a particular kind of society in Australia.

But whereas this nineteenth-century idea of China was by distant proxy, because we had not much direct experience of it and only knew it through Chinese people arriving on our shores, several matters of huge import after World War II—communism in China, the Korean War, the Malayan Emergency, the Cold War, Vietnam—brought China much closer and more directly into our focus, until it became something of a political preoccupation. Of course Australians in the 1950s didn't wake up thinking, my God, what are we going to do about China? Foreign issues were not such a constant in the public consciousness of Australian politics, and were brought forward mainly at election time. And almost no one actually went to China to be able to know what it was like. So China itself was still at one remove.

But China as a symbol was quite central. It was a measure of where you stood on what mattered, on what you wanted for Australia. In important ways it wasn't about radicals versus conservatives, or the Left versus the anti-communists. It was about those who wanted an identity for Australia based on an idea which belonged to another world and a connection with that other world, with Britain, which was receding, versus those who believed in a new idea for Australia, a new future and a new kind of culture. They did not want—or only a handful wanted—the politics of communism. They wanted a new kind of society.

Sir Robert Menzies—prime minister, Anglophile, monarchist, and aspirant to membership of a foreign parliament, the House of Lords—felt, I believe, threatened by China. Not because it could possibly have threatened us militarily, which he knew, but because of the idea which the new China embodied: an idea of a world which accepted Asians as having a rightful place in the sun, which accepted throwing out of Asia colonial powers including Britain, which admitted into the company of nations people who did not defer to whites, to the British throne or to the European societies fondly believed to be 'older' and 'more civilised'. This threatened what Menzies identified with and wanted to preserve for Australia. Not just

Menzies. Many Australians at the time still felt comfortable with Britain, even if it was becoming less relevant to their everyday lives, and many still referred to it as 'home'. But I don't think people realised how much Menzies wanted a Britannia-centred Australia and how much this influenced what he did in political life. He and people like him found nothing odd in wanting a permanent identity as crypto-Britons, middle-class Melburnians aping the manner of the British ruling class, and not even admitting Britons of Jewish origin to the Melbourne Club.

Many went along with Menzies' Britishism, and with the cleverly nurtured idea of the internal threat of communism, and the linking of this to the notion of the threat from China. And it was not only the comfortably off: working-class people who wouldn't have been allowed even to loiter in upper Collins Street went along with this linkage. Australians set to and strengthened the fortress of White Australia to keep the bastards out. They sought defence arrangements to keep China as far from Australia as they could. While ANZUS was originally directed at a possible resurgence of Japanese militarism, it became the cornerstone of Australian alliance policy against China. From 1954 it was buttressed by the broader anti-China alliance of SEATO, the South-East Asia Treaty Organisation. Australia sent troops to keep China at bay, directly and by proxy, in Korea and Malaya and Indo-China. And China became very central both in our foreign relations and domestically in keeping the Labor Party, the guilt-by-association Reds, out of office.

In this sense, Menzies set his face almost totally against Asia. He was a man on a life-support system from a receding world. History, in the longer judgment, will see him as having drugged much of Australia into similar unconsciousness, and the potion was the poison of what he called 'the downward thrust of China between the Indian and Pacific Oceans'.

Patrick FitzGerald, who *had* been to China, and did know what it was like, and was intellectually alive and independent, could be both conservative and also want a different identity for Australia. He was not, of course, wanting communism in Australia or anything like it. Nor was he wanting Sinicisation or Asianisation of our society. But his calls for diplomatic recognition did demand a self-recognition more profound, of an identity and a future by reference to things other than Britain and the Royal Family. Patrick was also a great lover of things

British and European, of Italian life and culture. But for Australia to have accepted his advocacy of China, in this broader sense, would have required a substantial realignment of our intellectual and cultural horizons. This was too much for most Australians. He was a man before his time. He was unjustly branded with the mark of perfidy, and non-communists who joined in his advocacy were very few.

In the 1960s, however, the question of who we were as Australians, or the alternative to crypto-Britannia, began to stir on a much wider front. And China was there again, at the centre. Menzies departed. And perhaps more importantly, Calwell departed. The Vietnam War came. Whitlam came. China was not the centre of Whitlam's foreign policy, but recognition of China was for him a central symbol not just of a new foreign policy but also of a very new kind of Australian society.

Where you stood on the Vietnam War, in the second half of the 1960s, became a statement of where you stood on 'What kind of Australia?' Or it was itself an expression of how you saw your own identity as an Australian. It was now clear that those non-Communist Party people who had been opponents of official China policy were not Reds, and while the government persisted in its slur, it was now more difficult to make it stick.

The 1960s were different from the 1950s also in that the lines between the advocates of two different kinds of Australia, one British and one Australian, were now more clearly drawn, and people began to move from the former to the latter. Calwell, while still leader of the Opposition, had actually supported the Vietnam War. With the passing of Calwell, those who supported the war by and large also stood for no change in the Australian symbols or culture. But if you were against the war, you tended to be concerned with how we saw ourselves. You wanted reflection, self-examination, and change. Many wanted independence for Australia. You didn't want the ideas or the priorities of somewhere else, some other government. You wanted your own. You therefore had to challenge, to stand up to the bludgeoning arguments of the United States, to assert something else, something that was Australian. And that, if you dared, led you to question a lot of other things, like Britain, the Royal Family, the white Australian genocidal acts against Aboriginal society.

Two related things began to happen in the 1960s. One was that a few people began studying China on a broader and often more contemporary front. This was the decade of the new China programs at Melbourne University and the Australian National University. This was the decade of Gregory Clark, who spoke Chinese and knew enough about China to challenge the conventional China wisdom of government. Patrick FitzGerald, scholar, intellectual, publicist (and beautiful prose stylist), now had allies and supporters. And they were no longer just the few non-communists in the Australia–China Friendship Society (the communists being little more than mouthpieces of the Chinese Communist Party in Beijing).

The other was that more people actually went to China: Wheat Board and Wool Board; businessman and scientist; student and medico; Tom Uren and Francis James. And so did I. While I would have considered myself an anti-conservative at university in the late 1950s, and anti-monarchist, like quite a number of people of my age and background, I came to the real awakening of myself as an Australian, an Australian Australian, through the processes of broad politicisation of Australian society of the 1960s, in which the Vietnam War was a central element. And so was China, and in my case also the study of China and the direct exposure to it.

Learning Chinese was important. It was still rare enough in Australia to cause comment and the constant urging, 'Go on Fitzie, say something in Chinese'. (What did one say? Mostly I counted to ten, or recited a line from the many I had to commit to parrot memory for the weekly tests at Point Cook.) But later, in Hong Kong, the very effort of having to leave my own culture in order to get far enough inside Chinese culture to be able to speak and understand the language forced me into some new consciousness of my own culture and my own society. When I returned to Australia at the end of that time, in late 1965, I was Australia-sensitised, even if still unversed in Australian politics and very young. But when my wife and I arrived late in Sydney from Hong Kong and took the night train to Melbourne and opened the curtains at dawn to a December sunlit plain, I found with thumping emotion how much I loved Australia. We both found. In a way, I had come to love China. But I cared passionately for Australia.

I first met Whitlam in early 1967. Beyond the introductions, he didn't speak until he'd ordered his lunch, and then he turned to me and said, 'I love food!' I knew we would get on. He saw, not in China but reflected in the China issue, many of the issues he was articulating: China as connected with the war; the war as connected with our relations with the United States, and therefore also with our independence. China had been connected by his political opponents with the domestic politics of elections from the time he had entered Parliament. Because of the way in which the conservatives had used the issue to keep Labor out of office, it had also washed over into broader electorate perceptions of Labor as an alternative government. It was divisive.

China was many other things to Whitlam. It was part of the Third World. It was asserting its independence. So were most of the countries of the Asian region. So did Whitlam seek to do for Australia. He saw a similarity of aspiration between his kind of Australia and the Asian neighbours. And such a society had to be self-conscious about its vision, its goals, its independence, its culture.

He was not obsessed by China. It was not his main preoccupation; in office, many other things occupied him in foreign policy. But it was very important to him and one of the major symbols of his political life. He had a determination to overturn the ethos of what he saw as a very non-Australian culture: the Australia conservatives had wanted to place in cultural formaldehyde. He always said, and he said it to Chou En-lai when we went there while he was still in opposition in 1971, that his first act as prime minister would be to establish diplomatic relations with China. In the event, his first act was to form a two-person Cabinet, but we did meet about China on the Sunday afternoon after the Saturday election, and the instructions went to the Embassy in Paris on the Monday.

After my meeting with Whitlam in 1967, and a few more which followed, I went off to Hong Kong again for a year, and on to a heady trip to Cultural Revolution China. Heady partly because I nearly lost my head to Red Guards in Changsha. If I had ever thought China might be a tempting system politically, my friend and sometime 'treasurer' Jack Harris likes to relate that the first words I spoke when I got off the train from China in Kowloon in February 1968 were 'Thank God for capitalism'.

I came back to Australia in 1968 to the thunder of the storm against the Vietnam War. Those who were marching against the war, which was said to be the downward thrust of China, were many of them new to protest—not the socialist Left, not just the Left, not even just Labor voters, but a broad section of those who were responding to the same impulses as Whitlam to reassess and define our own society. And the China issue now lay across a much more polarised party-political divide. Those who marched were the people who would ultimately come to vote for Whitlam when, with the whiff of victory in its nostrils after the 1969 election, Labor cleaned up Victoria and readied itself for government. These were the people who wanted an end to censorship (remember the banned books?), the new women, the republicans, the nationalists of film and television and the arts, the conservationists and the concerned scholars. They were drawn into one burgeoning stream which debouched into the streets and ultimately into the national tally room on election night, 2 December 1972.

It may have been Jim Cairns, demagogue, who marched at the head of the biggest demo Melbourne had ever seen. Whitlam was uncomfortable with people chanting 'We don't want your fucking war'. But it was Whitlam, intellectual, man of culture, who really understood what it meant to be a pilgrim. It was Whitlam who understood and articulated in the political sense the meaning of the China issue in the culture of Australia and turned it to good use in the pilgrimage for rediscovery of the Australian identity.

And Whitlam, of course, went to China in 1971, before the election and before Kissinger, against the tide, against the advice of many of his colleagues but at the urging of Mick Young, himself one of those in the 1950s who had made the journey and returned committed to an Australian vision for Australia. Whitlam and Young are in the pantheon of 'Australians in China', not because they were politicians but because, whatever influence China may have had on them, they had the capacity to influence the whole of Australia.

Whitlam did not radicalise Australia, or even the Australian middle class. He Australianised it. The 1972 election was a great national catharsis, and the recognition of China was a part of this great national release. One of the most persistently divisive issues for more than twenty years was now purged from Australian politics, and has not returned since as a partisan issue.

Now everyone wanted to go to China, and nearly everyone did. The Australian face in China was now a different one, and often with something specific to do, something to build, and captivated by what it found. People came back to build China in to whatever they did in normal life in Australia. Former deputy prime minister and Country Party leader Doug Anthony went, and found that he did not, as he had warned in 1971, have to fear for the safety of his children. Queensland's Bjelke-Petersen went, and found them 'very Christian' in their morality. Like him, it was said. By the end of the decade it was often quipped that the real distinction was if you hadn't been to China.

China was part of our 1970s. And Australians' discovery of China was part of the joyful discovery of themselves throughout most of the decade.

I missed the Whitlam years, because I was in China. I came back only once, briefly in early 1975, when Jim Cairns and Juni Morosi were the gossip and Gough paid no heed because he said he wouldn't listen to gossip. I had been away more than two years. I went from lunch with Gough and Margaret into a newsagent's in Canberra and picked up a magazine. It was titled *Dick*, and subtitled *The Magazine with Balls*. Australia had changed.

I think the momentum by the mid-1970s was building towards something very new and very different in Australia, which would have given us a sense of vision and purpose and self-knowledge about where we wanted to go, and what we had to do with our society to make it better, and what we had to do in our relations with the rest of the world—a sense of purpose and confidence in our own culture.

The economic failure of the Whitlam Government did not matter in this regard. It had shown us a way to find our own culture and we were rejoicing in it. China wasn't central to that by any means, nor should it have been. But as cultural identity is both about what you are and what distinguishes you from what you relate to, relating to China was part of this process of self-discovery, and in our foreign policy there was nothing quite as exciting. It was for the tens of thousands of Australians who went there a discovery of entirely new perceptions, and one of these was that there are more things in heaven and earth than Britain and America.

There was also the discovery which is that of the child when it suddenly finds there is something in its environment it can control, and thereby grows in personality and self-confidence. We had gone against the United States and the sky had not fallen. We went on to go against it in Vietnam and still the sky remained suspended. We could do Australian things, as we had done with China, and then with other neighbours. We could define ourselves as we wanted to and in relation to our Asian neighbours, who were our new points of reference. And then it came undone, and the vision and self-knowledge became confused and then lost, and China in the 1980s became central again in some ways that were very negative.

'AUSTRALIA'S CHINA'

What happened? If we had started with a sense of history and perspective we seemed to have lost both. We seemed to have no judgment. Whitlam had been intellectual about China, but Whitlam had gone, and in those who followed the intellectual arguments about China were lost in what became part Shangri-La, part goldrush. Like the dreams of huge money that so magnetised some business and political leaders, China itself became a dream, and ultimately an illusion, of expectations which had no foundation and which China could not possibly have fulfilled. We spoke of the time since 1972 as the time of 'normalisation'. But the 1980s seemed abnormal. If Whitlam's intention in 1972 had been to achieve balance in our approach to the region of Asia, in the 1980s we often seemed to achieve imbalance because of the obeisance we seemed to make to China, alone among Asian countries. Australians almost competed with each other in doing China things. And much of what was done was done with some kind of illusion of China in mind, some fantasy of our own creation, albeit often fostered by some in China.

I have a commitment to the relationship with China, and few have been more involved in it over the last few decades. I have enough documented and anecdotal material to fill a couple of theses or a dozen novels. I have spent hundreds of recorded days with Australians in China situations, with ministers and other politicians, with people in the arts and education, research and science and technology and sport, in fashion and gastronomy, and in whatever else you care to name; and with perhaps several hundred leading businessmen from Australian companies. The deference, breathless admiration and even sycophancy of the 1980s was daily fare. And although by the 1980s I had nothing to do with the government's China policy and was not even close to those who had responsibility for it (and was even held at arm's length by some politicians who resented Whitlam and by some officials who had opposed my appointment as ambassador), these attitudes were of deep and growing concern to me because in the long term they were damaging to our relations with China. The infatuation was unmatched in our relations with any other country, but it was not remotely supported in scale, breadth, depth, enthusiasm or resources by teaching of the language and society of the country with which we had become so enchanted.

Nor was this a phenomenon of what went into the decision to recognise China in 1972. After Whitlam, it became a protracted affair on a national scale which began in the late 1970s. Bettina Arndt observed wryly in 1977 that in terms of interest and excitement in the Australian popular mind China had come to equal sex, and that the two together ought to be a winning combination on lecture platforms around the country.

By the 1980s China became almost obligatory for government ministers. It wasn't just that they hadn't been there before. Most of them hadn't been to Indonesia either, or anywhere else in Asia, and many never did go. In the life of one government, it was joked that all but the Minister for Veterans' Affairs had been to China. Even the Minister for Police had been. Ministerial visits require things to talk about. So initiatives were born in China, sometimes for no other reason, which might have served us better in other parts of Asia had we gone there instead.

Not a few ministers found it difficult or impossible to say anything unpalatable to Chinese in this decade. Although by then not in government, I have known briefings for ministers leading business or cultural or educational delegations to China where it was agreed that there were difficult issues to be firmly addressed but which were forgotten when it came to the point in discussion. One former minister went to China and commended the Chinese bureaucracy (60 million of them, notorious among Chinese for being obstructive, conservative, inefficient and time-serving) as superior to our own in loyalty, efficiency, responsiveness and selflessness! Canberra saw as many as five or six ministers at informal dinners at the Chinese Embassy, when ambassadors from other important Asian countries could not even get one minister to a National Day reception.

In the language of government, China was often ascribed a measure of importance whose centrality was obvious but whose justification was difficult to see, particularly in economic matters. For more than a decade there was actually a government unit set up for the purpose of assisting the Chinese to sell to us. Large amounts of public money were spent on our own trade efforts in China, for unspectacular returns. We put almost nothing into economic relations with Taiwan, and yet, in many of these years, the volume of trade with Taiwan rivalled or exceeded trade with the People's Republic of China.

Hundreds of companies which had never set foot outside Australia chose China, a daunting market at the best of times, for their first attempt. Companies which had never joint-ventured in Australia set off to do so in China. Australian firms gave to China technology they would not sell elsewhere. Public and private sector interests even combined in amazing favours to China in tax concessions and concessional finance. China business seminars proliferated to the point of hypnosis. One prominent Australian businessman came back and revealed that Mao Zedong was comparable to Jesus Christ!

A similar phenomenon overtook academia. All manner of tertiary institutions signed up for exchanges or institutional links with China on the basis of two-way benefit, even when the benefit was clearly one way. At faculty boards which normally inspect at length and with scepticism the curriculum vitae of candidates from a good university in India or Taiwan or Indonesia, PhD scholarships were awarded to people from China with no degree at all, often an interpreter encountered on a trip.

Since 1978 I have been constantly in China—sometimes as often as ten or a dozen times a year and for up to a third of my working year—and I once started counting the number of people I travelled with in China who, while expressing negative views about Japanese, Indians, Pakistanis, Koreans and Indonesians, but particularly Japanese, had the most glowing things to say about Chinese in general and the most creative positive judgments to offer about particular Chinese individuals. The numbers were running at about nine in every ten. What kind of Wonderland was this? What kind of people could be so unflawed? And one wondered what on earth these Australians had in their minds when they thought of China, and what effect this had on their decision-making.

Some, mainly in business, became sceptical as the 1980s wore on. But it was uncertain whether this scepticism came from realism about China or from the general sense then developing in Australian business that Asia was too hard and it was easier to do business in America.

To a country which was very important, we as a nation now gave exaggerated importance. To a country which deserved our attention, we attended in such concentration as often to neglect other, equally deserving countries in Asia. To intelligent and tough-minded leaders in a tough political system we ascribed such qualities of intellect, sophistication and political durability as to blind us to history and human and political frailties and the inevitability of the passing of individuals from the continuing scene of government. Into a country of significant future economic and trade potential we put more public and private sector money and effort than into all the other new growth economies of Asia combined, and we endowed it with a capacity to respond to and satisfy our economic needs which would have been publicly challenged on all fronts if it had been held seriously of any other country. To a system which had done its best to reduce one of the glories of Chinese culture, cuisine, to an undistinguished base for a monosodium glutamate sauce, we paid tribute for the world's great culinary experience. To a people truly deserving our friendship and support, we bent over forwards in indecent enthusiasm. To a government which warranted the respect deserving of a Great Power and regional neighbour, we were at times in a posture which a Chinese official once characterised to me as 'ke tou', better known in English as 'the kowtow'.

Many Australians involved in the relationship actually believed hints dropped carefully into conversations by Chinese officials that China's relationship with us was qualitatively different from its relations with most others. Not exclusive, but somehow special to us in preference to other countries, often named, such as Japan. To these Australians, China was 'our China'.

And so it went until June the fourth, 1989, when the mindlessness of what had been going on was thrown suddenly into relief.

There is, of course, a fascination and seduction in the China experience which is almost universal. It is not just Australian. It obviously has something to do with the things that assail the senses, particularly food, and the culinary culture of China. It also has to do with Chinese music, and the tonal sounds of Chinese speech; with the originality of Chinese writing, and with architecture and painting instantly recognisable the world over as Chinese. This fascination is also carefully fostered by some official Chinese (almost anyone with a 'position' in China then was 'official', even in universities). Chinese have innate skills at persuading foreigners of how different China is and at

verbally and fulsomely rewarding them for small steps in understanding. Part of this is that foreigners can never understand
China. 'Ah, but you do not understand China' is a statement
delivered with a finality intended to confound all further argument. Foreigners, particularly Western foreigners, are thereby
often drawn to know more, to understand fully.

But there was a distinctively Australian affliction, which
had to do with the naiveté of ruling elites in Australia, perhaps
the innocence of the leaders of a New World country in encounter with countries and cultures of the Old World. It had always
been the case that white Australia had found it difficult to have
an easy relationship with Asian countries and peoples. Unsubtle
attitudes and emotions had long characterised national
approaches to our neighbours: fear, aggression, condescension,
insecurity, over-friendliness in its patronising and servile forms,
possessive paternalism, and the possessive arm of 'mateship'
around an unreciprocating Asian shoulder. We projected onto
Asians images of our creation, categorised them into stereotype.
The stereotypes were beginning to break down in the 1980s, but
Asia was still so little noticed in the Australian classroom that
our education was doing hardly anything to accelerate this
process.

The Asian immigration debate of 1988 illustrated how widespread and deep-rooted these stereotypes were. It was in fact
immigration, or rather the immigration inquiry in which I was
involved in 1988, which exposed to me some aspects of the
behaviour of Australian political elites which seemed to explain
something also about their attitudes to Asia. It seemed to me
that the history of immigration, and settlement philosophy, had
been a history of Commonwealth and State politicians walking
backwards, of step-by-step-backwards decision-making in reaction to representation, pressure, threat and manipulation by
immigrant spokespeople. Many of the decisions may have been
right ones, but they weren't decisions of initiative, of people in
intellectual or cultural control, working within some kind of
vision or to some forward-thinking plan. And as immigration
from the mid-1950s slid to the periphery of government concerns
and became more about dealing with immigrants than about
dealing with a major national policy issue, the interaction with
immigrant leaders became the most important determinant in
immigration policy.

The Anglo and Celtic political elites of this country often
found it acutely difficult to deal with the people from the old

societies from which our immigrants had come. Their foreign-ness was awkward for the immature and unsophisticated. They were also seen as wily and manipulative and duplicitous. They were undeterred by countless knock-backs, which their self-interest and survival dictated and which in their home societies were part of politics. The naive politicians of the Australian New World spoke pejoratively of them behind their backs, but were repeatedly manoeuvred, and mostly did not understand. If they did understand, in their naiveté they were psychologi-cally and culturally out of their depth and therefore often felt inferior; they wanted to placate, to please, to be liked. And being liked by immigrant groups was what came to dictate immigration and migrant settlement philosophy.

The same inexperienced innocence, the same closed men-tality, the same desire to please, infected our dealings with Asian countries. These were not the only reason we became besotted with China in the 1980s, but our fascination for China was lethal when combined with our ignorance and the reality of our economic and geopolitical situation.

When China ceased being the enemy and became 'our friend', we leapt into euphoric expectation. As the 1980s found us more alone internationally than ever before, we became ever more abandoned in courtship of China. Government attitudes were bolstered by public perceptions, and in business and in academia, we simply did not know how to handle ourselves when confronted close up with this most ancient and manipu-lative of societies. We were insecure. We were awkward and often gauche. There was little sense of wisdom or maturity or simple hard-headedness. And because we wanted to be liked, we tended not to drive a hard bargain, we tended to be soft, to give in, to accept the Chinese proposition about 'equality and mutual benefit' in a relationship that was patently often neither equal nor mutually beneficial.

'They like us!' people exclaimed. How distinctive it was to be liked by such distinctive people.

Some would argue that the huge investment of effort in China in the 1980s paid off. It's not easy to see how. We had a good relationship with China, with, until 4 June 1989, no major points of friction between us. Perhaps we ought to have had more issue than we did with China, on nuclear weapons, for example, or Hong Kong, Tibet, human rights. Our good relationship was in part due to our placating on sensitive issues.

Would we have done the same then with Indonesia? Or Fiji? Or France?

We had an expanding economic relationship. We talked on many matters and sometimes caucused together in international forums. We often talked constructively about closer political and economic development of the Asian region.

This was all excellent. But did it exceed the normal expectations of a bilateral relationship? Was it commensurate with the weight we gave it and the effort we expended? I think not. We might say we were building credit for the future, but there was no evidence that we even thought about the future. We might argue that China's extremely mild response to Australia's official and popular outrage over Tiananmen Square proved that our policies paid off by way of a relationship able to withstand such trauma. We did have a reasonable underlying relationship, but it's also the case that China's responses to criticism of June the fourth were strongest where it saw its interests most strongly affected—in Hong Kong, for example, or the United States. I also wonder if China's mildness over our condemnation of the massacre was a distinction to be welcomed. Do we want to be indulged because we are believed to be compliant? I recall a Chinese tourism official once saying that China preferred Australian tourists because they were so 'obedient'! That is not a judgment I would welcome on Australia as a nation.

It was of course necessary to have a correction to the consequences of having had 22 years of China as the enemy. But while we developed some scepticism about China after June the fourth, what was missing was an intellectual reassessment, unbound by the assumptions of the previous decade and a half, freewheeling, self-interested, culturally and intellectually sophisticated, well informed through proper understanding of Chinese society, and psychologically mature. To do that we would have had to start with an examination of the underside of the relationship.

I believe in the upside, soberly addressed. I would not otherwise have given or continue to give a large part of my career to advancing our relations with China. But the downside is that we have no special relationship with China, as we have none with any country in Asia, in the sense that we used to have once with Britain or the United States. We have the Chinese ear on some things, but little demonstrable influence. And China owes us few favours. For all the favours we have bestowed on China, we have received few in return, although

Chinese acts of self-interest, like their major investments in Australia, were often greeted with wonderment and acclaim, as though they were favours.

We have in fact often encouraged the Chinese to take advantage of us in the political and diplomatic relationship, in business, in cultural relations, in aid, in most of our dealings, and to this extent almost all of what I have described above is our fault, not China's.

But let me give one small illustration of what happens, and which encapsulates some of our problems. It was decided in the mid-1980s to establish in China at Australian cost a wool warehouse. The Chinese were enthusiastic. It was originally to serve a number of purposes, including display of Australian wool types, and through demonstration of modern handling and distribution to improve the throughput of wool and thereby to assist in the development of wool use in China, which China wanted, and the promotion of Australian wool. It was to be Australian-managed. The negotions were protracted, even though, as a gift, there ought not to have been too much to negotiate.

It's not the fact that the warehouse ended up in Nanjing instead of Shanghai, through which most imported wool is distributed. It's not even the fact that with a shameless greed which Australian taxpayers who paid for this warehouse would find stunning, the Chinese parties demanded more, and then more, and then more. It was that when they did not get their way, the negotiators shouted, ranted, were abusive and insulting. On one occasion the insults became so bad that the then chairman of the Australian Wool Corporation, in China for goodwill and not negotiation, had to be withdrawn from the meeting room and a subsequent apology extracted via the State Economic Commission. On another, a senior Australian official, the redoubtable Dr Jocelyn Chey, rose to the insinuations of the officials and expostulated, 'What do you think we are! Spies!' When completed, the warehouse carried mainly non-Australian wool. It was not Australian-managed. Australian officials were denied access to it. This was not the Cultural Revolution. It was not a commercial deal. It was not in a commodity peripheral to our interests but in wool, one of the significant stories in our economic relations.

Shocking as this may seem, it ought not to surprise. I have never been in a Canberra office where Australian officials have shouted abuse at foreign negotiators, but I have seen Chinese do so. When some Chinese interlocutors do not get their way, they may use threats and intimidation, ranging from the blunt to the highly subtle. The latter, at political and diplomatic and economic policy levels, effectively stalled the proper development of legitimate Australian commercial interests in Taiwan, including the establishment of air links.

I pay tribute to the many Chinese friends and officials who have stood against this kind of attitude and for a relationship of real equality. When I spoke publicly on these matters in 1989, some Chinese were upset that I had spoken openly about them. Most did not understand that this was not prompted by June the fourth but by a concern about a tendency in our relationship which had been going on throughout the 1980s and which I had spoken of at a public forum in Beijing in 1984 and again in 1985, and that the point of my 1989 criticism was directed at Australia.

If we stand firm in our own interests, there is no problem. If we comply, we do ourselves a disservice and encourage some Chinese to have misplaced expectations. If we are thought to be generally compliant and then try to take a stand, the expectations are denied and tension and hostility ensue.

Our relationship with China in the 1980s was dangerous not only in its own terms but also for the way in which it skewed our relations with the rest of Asia. There was serious neglect of Japan, and during one Japanese prime ministerial visit to Australia, Japanese officials could only react with dismay at our apparent 'China preoccupation' and the offhand nature of the Australian reception. Bridges to Indonesia, which screamed for attention, were in the early 1980s barely on anyone's agenda, and the whole relationship was then allowed to slide into a state of neglect which was extraordinary given that Indonesia is our closest neighbour, and a very significant country. And Indo-China. Had we not been so susceptible to Chinese influence, would we have found it so difficult in those years to have a close relationship with Hanoi? Would we have so unreservedly condemned the Vietnamese invasion of Cambodia?

The irony is that we did not learn the lesson. Since 1989 we have been through a major infatuation with Indonesia and some minor ones elsewhere—in Thailand, for example, and Vietnam. The scale has not been comparable, but the lack of history, and the lack of a sense of history, has been much the same.

THE AFTERMATH OF JUNE THE FOURTH

Did we not become intelligent about China after the spell was broken on June the fourth, 1989? Our attitudes were laid bare by the surprise we felt at having been 'betrayed', as some of our political and business leaders put it. Betrayed? Had we so possessed China that we had been betrayed? What pact of love or commitment on China's part had promised that something like this could not happen? But did we change? Even in our reaction we still showed the same favouritism towards China. To what other country in turmoil and oppression have we extended such a mass act of grace as we extended to the 28 000 Chinese who happened to be in Australia at the time?

We can have a normal and healthy and reasonably equal relationship, but there are two problems which have to be addressed if we are to do so. The first is to educate ourselves about China. If China is so important, why is it still the case that only one member of the national Parliament speaks Chinese? The second problem is the history. June the fourth should not have been a surprise if we had seen that the potential for such behaviour was there. In the 1980s the rhetoric of communist ideology was set aside and China began to deal more directly with its real problems, but it was still not apparent that paternalistic, authoritarian and despotic approaches to government had disappeared. So we have to concentrate very hard on developing the skills and capacities of our people. For this we need commitment of resources. If we'd put all the money that went into the 1980s China Action Plan into the training of teachers and other China professionals, we would have had more sanity in our China policy in the 1980s and would have more dollars earned in the 1990s than all the China economic initiatives will ever produce.

It is not possible to have a fixed or unchanging view of China because it is not only a complex society, it is more a world than a country. Many Chinese demand a kind of all-or-nothing 'friendship' from foreigners, but that is seldom possible and in any event ought not to be possible or appropriate with any country. Most foreign China specialists, especially those who have been through the mill of learning Chinese, feel the magnetic fascination of China, but most also come to have ambivalent views about it. Most critics have been enthusiasts or may be critical on some things but supportive on others. Even some of the most eloquent early Western critics of the

Cultural Revolution in China had themselves started out with positive views of that movement. The enthusiasm for China, followed by the scepticism, is something most of us have experienced; and I have been wrong in judgments and have had to change my mind on some critical issues and events. This has been a salutary experience, and it is partly from this experience that I judge what happened nationally in the 1980s. What is important here, however, is that we must have the capacity to change our minds, and also to go on learning. To do that nationally, we have to start learning.

In China itself, our focus should also be on education, as an instrument of policy. The advantages are obvious. The education and training of people is of great benefit to China. And for us, if a woolstore is filled with Argentinian wool, at least some of the corridors of China would be filled with the products of Australian education. Then, if we care, for example, about the state of the free expression of ideas in China, what better way to express this concern than through education? The same arguments can be made about our dealings with some other Asian societies, but in China they are pressing. And it is essential that they be seen as central to policy, and not as secondary or incidental.

Patrick FitzGerald would never have advocated what went on in the 1980s. But then, he was a historian.

But where did it all end up, the connection on which he started out in the 1950s, between China and domestic Australian society, and the Australian identity? If where Australians stood on China in the 1950s was a statement about Australian society then, this was also true, at times spectacularly, in 1980s Australia, which I will come back to in Chapter 8. Our approach to China in the 1980s also defined our approach to Asia in general, which in turn landed us in the predicament we face in Asia in 1997.

CHAPTER 3

The Asianisation of Asia

It was not so much the failure to anticipate ASEM but the failure to see the phenomenon which produced it that was so seriously wrong about the Australian idea of what was going on in Asia in the 1990s. Had we been open to other perspectives, we might have seen the significance for us of this development when it began, in the southeast part of East Asia, back in the late 1960s and early 70s.

This phenomenon consisted of East Asian states talking to each other collectively and doing things collectively, *without* Western presence, participation, or initiative. This was new, at least in modern times. There had been systems of international relations in Asia before the Europeans. These had been largely interdicted by European colonial occupation, to the extent that at the time of decolonisation after World War II the directional flows of trade, politics and people of most East Asian states were not with each other but with the metropolitan colonial headquarters in Britain, Europe and the United States. So deeply had colonial division severed the links within the region that it was commonly held by Westerners that there could never be an Asian Community, like the European, because Asian countries had far too many cultural and other differences to be able to reconcile them.

The European and American part in their separation was of

course not acknowledged. But the intellectual and psychological impact on Asian elites themselves was profound. They knew almost nothing of each other, their education was generally devoid of Asian content, and most of them also agreed with the contention that Asia was too diverse to form an Asian Community.

From small beginnings in the 1960s and 70s, multilateral discussions, forums and arrangements internal to the region and excluding Europeans and Americans began to proliferate in the 1980s. There was no one organisation or even impetus. There was necessity, where for example governments had to talk to each other about common problems. There was spontaneity, in business, and sport, and leisure. And in some quarters there was a more explicit agenda for formal cooperation, notably in ASEAN, the Association of Southeast Asian Nations, which was inaugurated in August 1967.

Defining this phenomenon was not at first an issue, as it evolved unevenly and sporadically, and Asian 'style' tended to require that issues of explicit definition should not be forced. But by the end of the 1980s it was very clear that here was something distinctly 'Asian': in East Asia, and neither European nor American. What it represented was a new Asianness, and a new and powerful process in East Asia—Asianisation, the Asianisation of Asia.

It is difficult to comprehend how Australian elites, including those engaged in our relations with Asia, failed to see the significance of this phenomenon, for East Asia and for Australia, and even denied its existence. I have sat in the presence of intelligent Australians who 'asked' intelligent Asians about the main game in East Asia, usually in something like the following way:

— This so-called Asianisation is not the issue, is it?
— No (politely).
— Asian states are more interested in collaboration with North America, aren't they?
— Yes (more politely).
— We are all converging, aren't we?
— Of course (very politely).
— (To me) You see, he agrees.

It is ironic also that at the very time when Australian elites were beginning to realise the diversity of Asia and were earnestly telling each other that there was not one Asia but many,

what was emerging in the region was the beginnings, if not of
one Asia, at least of an Asian Community in part of Asia.

WHAT IS ASIANISATION?

Some time ago I sat in the foyer of the Imperial Hotel in Tokyo
with Yoichi Funabashi, respected senior writer on foreign affairs
for the *Asahi* newspaper and now its bureau chief in Washington. I talked about the Asia–Australia Institute and its central
interest, the Asianisation of Asia. Funabashi did not find this
novel, and we discussed among other things a speech given
some time earlier by Fuji Xerox chairman Kobayashi, in which
he explored the 're-Asianisation' of Japan. Next day I met a
Japanese official who said to me with a mix of anger, condescension and fright: 'Asianisation does not exist! And if it did,
we must never use the term!'

Asianisation was not something on which people could
easily agree, although few in Asia would now deny that it exists.
Asianisation is ultimately a political thing, and as a defining
concept for what is happening in Asia the term is still unsatis-
fying to many, because in the age of economism we seem to
have tried to bury politics, when in fact it is at the root of
economic issues and at the heart of most international problems
and their solution.

For my part, I am talking to Funabashi and others about
this issue because I am trying to work out what is going to
happen to my own society over the next 30 years, politically
and socially, as well as economically. That is why I am centrally
interested in the Asianisation of Asia. Someone asked me if this
was not some kind of Australian obsession. In a way, for me,
it is. Australia faces a fateful choice about Asia. In the game
of self-identifying regions which is in play across the world, it
wants to be with Asia (however Australia understands it), and
it is with Asia that it has cast its lot.

More or less. The decision having been made, Australia is
nervous about it, in both semantics and substance. The Labor
Government danced in turn towards and away from definition
of being 'part of' Asia. The Coalition Government which came
to power in 1996, while publicly committed to Asia, says
emphatically that we are 'not Asian' and definitely not 'part of'
Asia. It hesitates, and looks back at a past Australia, and a
past world, in which there was 'certainty', no need to confront

difficult choices. And in most quarters in Australia there is little or no understanding of what commitment to Asia could mean for our society, beyond the economic benefits we can see under our noses.

But the decision is forced upon us and the choice is more or less made, and it is a political choice rather than an economic one. This choice is quite different from that which may be faced by the United States, for example, or Canada. It is difficult to think of any other country, perhaps any country in history, in which a nation's elites have knowingly committed themselves, not to join organisationally but possibly to become part of a region or 'world' whose dominant histories and cultures and ethical and value systems they do not understand. This is of course why we skirt around the commitment and try to contain and condition it semantically, something that does not go unnoticed in Asia.

So we, Australia, actually have to try to know what Asianisation, and 'Asian values', could mean, for us. Because it may mean more for us politically, by virtue of our predominantly Western background, than for any other country.

TENSIONS IN THE ASIANISATION DEBATE

Asianisation is a contested concept, in both Asia and the West, and it has many meanings. Although it is used by various groups in Asia and some governments to justify their exercise of political power, that does not invalidate its other meanings. In general, it is real and not imaginary or fabricated (as some Western commentators suggest), and at the least it is an expression of a feeling among Asian elites of confidence and pride in achievement, a sense of being 'empowered', of being 'Asian' in the way that elites in Europe have of being 'European', and a sense of having 'arrived' or 'rearrived'. It sometimes finds expression as the assertion of 'Asian values' (although that is not all it is about) and it is sometimes also expressed explicitly in resistance or, less often, in opposition to 'Western values'.

What has marked the discussion of this issue is the tension it creates, both between Asians, partly because it is probably the beginning of the real deciding game in how Asian states are going to come together politically and who will dominate, and also between Asia and the West, because (in my opinion) the

West does not like Asianisation or fears it or denies it or simply finds it extremely difficult to comprehend.

Asianisation is not therefore an easy matter to discuss (and this may be one reason why Dr Mahathir's version of it has had such a difficult time). I think this is because the word itself makes difference too explicit for many people from Asian cultures, exposes too much of what people on all sides of the issue really think. There is a tendency to push it away from being the central framework for discussion, to suggest that it is not an issue at all, or that it is not new, or that it has always been there and we should just get on with being Asian without talking about it.

It seems one often can discuss the theory of convergence without being uncomfortable in this way. The dominant ideas of convergence are of course overwhelmingly Western, as is commonly also the projected end point of the convergence process. One can comfortably discuss Asian cultures within the framework of Western convergence, but not so comfortably if the framework is Asianisation.

Why is this? There seem to be several broad reasons.

One is that in Western eyes, certainly, and in some Asian eyes also, the idea of Asianisation suggests concepts of race, and that is probably enough to make it uncomfortable, at least initially.

It is also cultural. Cultural challenge is difficult and can be threatening. If you set up Asianisation as the dominant framework for discourse about the Asian region, it tends to make explicit a challenge both to Western culture and to the convergence models of the West. Westerners resist it. And for reasons of Asian culture this is one reason why many Asians are reluctant to push it. Many Asians also fear that it will be misunderstood, or hold back from its use until its potency is known and they feel better prepared to manage what reaction might follow.

Another reason is that you can't talk about Asianisation without talking about its practical effect on relations between Asian states and the West, and in particular the United States. This is partly why my Japanese official friend was so jumpy about the concept, because if it is interpreted as implying that there is something which joins the countries of Asia and excludes others, this can be taken to mean 'drawing a line down the middle of the Pacific' and to suggest dichotomy rather than partnership, even if this is not what Asianisation is about. The

East Asian Economic Caucus (EAEC) of Dr Mahathir is one case where the exclusion has been made explicit, but while the EAEC draws on Asianisation, it is not its defining framework, and others involved in expounding Asianisation are less inclined to be confronting.

The question of the United States makes Asianisation a delicate matter in a practical and political sense. Not everyone in Asia likes to be as openly exclusive as Dr Mahathir, and even he plays the game of exclusion selectively. More commonly, from the Tokyo official who was terrified that the very mention of Asianisation in his presence might brand him as anti-American, to self-possessed and independent-minded officials in Kuala Lumpur or Jakarta, few in Asia believe it desirable, practical or wise to draw a line down the Pacific or provoke a new isolationism on the part of the United States.

Asianisation is a delicate subject also because it invites speculation about a possible Asian form of convergence, and hence the question: convergence under the dominance of whose ideas and whose culture? Dr Mahathir again provides the convenient reference; no other Asian country has been willing quite to let his idea be *the* defining concept for the Asianisation of Asia. This is also, of course, why some people hesitate to pursue the concept in a Japanese context, not for historical reasons (although these are also there in good measure) but because no one wants to contemplate an Asianised Asia under Japan's (or, for that matter, China's) cultural and political domination.

A fifth broad reason articulated by some is that even granted that Asianisation does exist, globalisation and a borderless world are more important and Asianisation is in conflict with these, and divisive. The real issue here, however, is that it is not a case of either/or. We are going to have both Asianisation and globalisation (and localisation besides, or 'glocalisation'), and the question is how are we going to manage all of these, because we have never had this before—it is utterly new.

I think it is also the case that Asian leaders have not until very recently been explicit in the use of this term when they talk among themselves. What brings it out is often some Western dismissal of the idea, or even simply some Western point of reference. At an Asia Leaders' Forum organised by the Asia–Australia Institute, at which this issue was the main item for discussion, there was an illustration of the latter process. What moved the discussion into explicit recognition of Asianisation was the invocation by one Asian speaker of those most Western of literary observers of the Asian world, E. M. Forster and Rudyard Kipling. The idea that 'never the twain shall meet' evokes so much of dated concepts of imperialism and colonialism and Western-owned dogmas about East and West that it cannot go unchallenged. It invites major questions. What is East and what is West? Has there always been East? What is East becoming? To what extent has East converged with West and does it want to? Who should set the terms? Almost without noticing, the participants at this forum slipped into a deep exploration of these issues within the framework of Asianisation and with the actual term 'Asianisation' as the common, if sometimes uneasy, point of reference.

PROCESS, STATE OF MIND, IDENTITY

The Asianisation of Asia is not, except in a utopian sense, a fusing into one Asian civilisation or amalgam of all Asian religions and cultures. Asianisation in Asia is a political force. It is a process, rather than something established, fixed or tangible. People use the words 'process', 'discovery', 'rediscovery', 'development', words suggesting movement, something in train, not complete. Asianisation is a real, elemental development, characterised by a sense of rearrival onto the world stage.

It is also a state of mind, largely cultural and social but in its expression also political. A perception or self-perception, an emotion, a sensation. It is about identity. Asianisation in Asian countries is about identity not only as Indonesian, for example, or Korean, but as *both* Indonesian or Korean *and* Asian. Like being European.

And Asianisation is now a political agenda, in different senses and in different mixes in different countries: in the sense of throwing down to the West a challenge of 'Asian values'; in the sense of an agenda to 'Asianise' Asia (as in the program of Dr Mahathir) and perhaps the world; and in the sense of using Asian values to create a sustaining 'ideology' for Asian ruling elites. This last tends to loom large in the minds of many in the West, which may obscure for them its other meanings and manifestations.

Asianisation is also an expression of cultural decolonisation. This may be one reason why it seems more vigorously expressed in the former colonies of Southeast Asia than in Northeast Asia, but the fact that in its broad social meaning it is cultural explains why it is right across the region, including in countries which were not colonies of the West. Political decolonisation was of course the necessary precondition. But it took the much more protracted process of economic decolonisation to create the psychological conditions for cultural decolonisation.

What exactly does cultural decolonisation mean? It means that just as the practice of economic development in Asia is no longer under the general tutelage of the West, neither is the way Asian elites think about the matters economic development is meant to address: the human condition itself, the social and cultural ends of economic development, and hence also values, ethics, rights, paths to political development and democratisation, everything to do with politics.

Even without an explicit political agenda, therefore, Asianisation puts politics back into politics, rescues it from the dominance of economics. But it is not just national. The shift to predominantly intra-Asian flows in trade and investment has brought Asians into direct partnership with each other, including between Southeast and Northeast Asia, and this has given the national experience of economic independence a sense of being a *shared* regional experience. And this has brought about a sense that the cultural and social experience of independence is also both national and regionally *shared*, 'Asian'.

The shared and even collective phenomenon fed by this daily intra-regional contact is also fanned by the extraordinary attention given by the Western-dominated international media to the region's economic performance, and the relentless use of the collective 'Asia' by the same media and the world's elites. It is not surprising that the self-confidence and self-esteem of the region's elites is drawn out into region-wide perspectives or that the spark leaps so readily across Asian national boundaries. The same international media which give so much attention to the economic forces driving the region, however, tend to miss or malign the equally potent cultural and political forces, as though the 'Asian' aspect of these forces does not exist or does not matter, or is simply about 'soft authoritarianism'—which it may sometimes be, but that misses the point.

The fact that so few Asian leaders speak directly to Westerners about Asianisation does not mean that it is not articulated. The problem for people from societies in the West, in which discourse tends to be direct and depends less on context and nuance, is that they often miss the more softly spoken or unspoken underlying themes in Asian discourse. And because they often also feel uncomfortable with the whole idea of Asianisation, they may tend to prefer interpretations which deny it, soften its challenge, and assert the inevitability of convergence into one fused global culture derived largely from Western-style democracy, Western values, Western culture, and Western languages.

Cultural decolonisation is also a state of mind. It is a cultural and political confidence which rests on economic self-assurance and a tacit, sometimes explicit, sense of solidarity with other Asians. It is a state of mind which does not accept without question, which says, 'I am going to talk about the fundamentals in my terms and I have a right to do so and I will not accept that the West has a right to deny this'. It is a state of mind which also says, 'We are Asians! It is good to be Asians. And what is more, the rest of the world says it is good to be Asians. Let us rejoice in this discovery and the discovery of each other!'

Among the expressions used about this state of mind is 'rediscovery of self' against the imposition of Western views, or a feeling of 'being able to express oneself again'. This idea of rediscovering the past, taking up the threads, resuming after the interruption of the colonial period, reaching back to what existed before the period of domination by Western ideas, is a strong explicit theme in the contemporary expression of this state of mind: 'We lost our Asian identity during colonialism but we have rediscovered it.' 'Asianisation has been there all along—it is simply a matter of going back to what one is.' 'Our Asian values have regained currency.' There is, however, some disagreement about the extent to which this is a rediscovery or an invention.

A third element of Asianisation, clearly linked with cultural decolonisation, concerns identity. This involves on the one hand reaching back into history and cultural roots, and on the other exploring what identity means in the new Asian cultural and political context. This process has a national dimension we are familiar with in many Asian countries, for example the constant articulation in China of 'Chinese characteristics'. But the daily use of the concepts Asian, Pan-Asian, Asianness, Asianisation has invited exploration of identity in a wider context, not unlike some of the debate which has taken place in Europe. The EAEC concept is an example, but it is present also in ASEAN, and in the less highly visible but immensely important non-government organisations which have proliferated across the region.

The identity issue is therefore also about creating a new identity, one that is 'Asian', which absorbs unthreatening parts of the West (Mozart and perhaps McDonald's), but may see others (liberal-democratic values) as a problem.

There is of course also a strongly reactive element in Asianisation which is fuelled by non-Asian powers. And the 'Asianised' state of mind is driven in part by the policy-focused debate which has been taking place in such contexts as APEC and the ASEAN Regional Forum. The question of cause and effect here is contested, but there is no doubt that in its reactive mode Asianisation is driven by accelerating internationalisation and by the intrusive projection of Western culture and values, or more particularly the 'popular' culture of the United States and what some describe as its more 'debased' values. Where westernisation impacts directly on Asian countries it produces a reflexive defence against this invasion of the mind and the senses, and drives some of the more explicit Asianisation agendas such as 'Asian values', which are discussed below.

(Significantly for Australia, all of the above—cultural decolonisation, soul-searching about identity, independence of mind, and concern about aspects of the Americanisation of our culture and society, and what these mean in the broad regional context—have been strong defining themes and elite preoccupations in Australia since the 1960s. While the starting-points may be different, on these fundamental issues we could have common ground, even if we do not see it.)

Asianisation is therefore also a kind of 'de-westernisation', like 'de-toxification', at least on such things as social, moral and political matters (in other respects, like consumerism related to Western products or the relentless pursuit of the growth doctrine of Western ideology, westernisation proceeds apace). And although the elites in most Asian countries tend to deny it, there is also a nationalistic element to Asianisation, including its reaction to westernisation. But if Asianisation were only about de-westernisation, it might find expression only in nationalism, which is clearly not the case. It is, as suggested above, more 'elemental', and just as clearly it resonates across the region of East Asia, beyond nationalism.

It may be that the next stage in the history of the region *will* see assertive and aggressive nationalism in Asian countries. Asia is not without its manifestations of this already, which I will come to later, and concern over the issue is already on the agenda in the private conversations and public forums of the region. So perhaps one of the great challenges for Asianisation is to find some way of ensuring that it does not engender in individual Asian countries an assertive and chauvinistic nationalism.

AGENDAS

Most East Asian governments have taken up Asianisation, explicitly and implicitly, and that puts culture back on the agenda. Or it may be more accurate to say that it puts culture back into economics, and politics back on the agenda, and elevates both culture and politics to a prominent place in government concerns.

Decolonisation by the colonised, from 'below' as it were, is not only *for* something, in this case an independence of mind and culture, but also *against* something. It therefore presupposes a continuing post-colonial presence and influence which in this case is Western, but because of the history of East Asia since the end of World War II, and perhaps unfairly, particularly American. Cultural decolonisation is a statement involving at its softest a questioning and at its hardest a resistance to the West in general and the United States in particular. It is a political statement.

How is it political? Some Asian leaders who are direct and explicit about the exclusivity of Asianness or Asianisation either imply or suggest directly a line which divides off the United States (and Australia). This is not necessarily a dividing line for economic or security purposes, and although difficult sometimes to understand the distinction, it is not usually *anti*-American. But it is certainly about power. Asian governments are engaged with this issue now because, with the removal of the defining ideological battle lines of the Cold War, they are seeking to define themselves against the power of the dominant ideology of the day, of the victors in the Cold War. Asianisation is about who in the next stage of human history dominates whom. It is about a contest of ideas: whose ideas will gain ascendancy, whose scholars' ideas will shape the world and give it coherence. Asianisation is part of a major historical shift in the world, anticipating a long period of decline in the United States.

But just as Asianisation cannot be discussed without reference to the United States, so also can it not be discussed without reference to China. And the discussion tends to end with a question mark over whether China sees itself as part of a regional process or just as China. The term 'domesticated' is often used by other Asians to describe how they would like China to be in regional affairs, but China's domestication is seen as by no means a foregone conclusion. It is something which needs to be 'managed' by China's neighbours. They acknowledge that they need to allow China the legitimate exercise of power internationally, while still being constrained and knowing its place. They say they need carefully to manage China's insertion into the modern world through regional associations. They must bargain with China, restrain China, but allow it to exercise its national sovereignty.

While China's neighbours do not see persuasive evidence that China is yet 'domesticated' to the region or a full partner in Asianisation, there is another (contested) view that what we fear about China—expansionism—is in fact a modern phenomenon and is not based in Chinese history, that it is a westernised China which would behave in ways which Western powers might behave, and therefore a westernised China which would be dangerous. If China follows Japan's modernisation example, Asia may be in trouble, but Asianisation can help restore the Asianness of China and help it reject Western values.

This argument puts an interesting Asian interpretation on the meaning of both historical West and historical China, but at the end of the day, in the contest of power the question mark over China remains.

One of the other great questions about Asianisation and power is whether an Asianised Asia will be exclusive or inclusive, competitive or cooperative. ASEM raises interesting questions in this regard, and brings the Asianisation discussion to the greatly contested issue of 'Asian values', a term which has excited more agitation than any other in use in this debate. Most of the agitation focuses on the *least* important aspect of this issue, which is whether the values frequently listed by Asian politicians (family, hard work, education, thrift) are Asian, or both Asian and Western, or universal. The most we can usefully say about this end of the debate is that both sides tend to be ahistorical (the Asian side ignoring that the West may once have valued these values more or had them as core—have they not heard of the 'Protestant work ethic'?—and the Western side ignoring that in the West's passage to today's societies the commitment to these values has undergone substantial mutation) and selective (the Asian side ignoring large sections of, for example, US society, in which these values are still core; and the Western side ignoring large sections of their own societies in which they are not).

There is not much enlightenment at this end of the Asian values debate. Most political leaders in Asia are the products of Western, modern, secular universities and have typically had no Asianised education in moral or religious values; they have not been taught Asian culture or literature for its inherent value. Most Western leaders who deny Asian values similarly have no learning in Asian culture. The debate is therefore superficial and often ill informed.

Beyond this superficial end of the debate, however, is the powerful function of the *idea* of Asian values as a significant connecting point and unifying concept for people in Asia seeking to define their Asianness and make some sense of what comes next when Western values are put at a distance or when the mix of Asian and Western values is significantly changed.

The idea of Asian values gives something to believe in, and this is essential to the stated goal of many Asian leaders of holding to core values as their economies modernise—in other words, avoiding going some of the ways of the West. 'The real issue is this: can we Asians successfully organise ourselves into the future? This is where the West has failed. Asianisation is about facing the challenge to construct an alternative arrangement suitable to our needs.'

In this limited sense, therefore, the ideology of Asian values is less important than the political function, which is, internally, to develop policies which it is hoped will avoid the social breakdown and decay seen to have been the fate of the West, and, regionally, to identify what it is Asian societies do have in common.

Asian leaders do not have at their disposal a great deal of research on differences between the values of Asian and Western societies, and most of the research that has been done is either Western or within the framework of Western ideas and methodology. But there is in fact more basis to the argument for an Asian weighting on the scale of values than the proponents themselves are sometimes able to adduce. As anthropologists, sociologists, linguists and others have observed, while all societies do have similar values and beliefs, they nevertheless place them in different orders of importance and emphasise some more than others. Certain values are regarded more highly, or

as 'core', in more collectivist societies than in more individualist societies. These values include, for example, harmony and
conflict avoidance, the importance of face and the public shame
of the loss of it, high context communication, emphasis on the
group and group orientation and differentiation, greater acceptance of 'power distance' or hierarchy, emphasis on virtue as
distinct from truth, attitudes to the law and the state.

There *is* distinction here between Asian societies and the
West even though there are of course collectivist societies in
parts of Europe. Given, however, that the distinction made by
Asian leaders often rests heavily on the example of the United
States, the distinction has genuine contemporary validity. It
also gives some substance to the argument that Asian values
have been around for a long time but have been obscured by
the fact that in modern times debate has been largely between
Western constructs (e.g. liberalism versus Marxism).

The argument of history, however, has also produced what
might once have been seen as a very Western fallacy, and this
is the creation of an ideal, romanticised self-image; in this case
a mythologised Asia, past and present, that overlooks Asian
problems, Asian exploitation, oppression, corruption, moral
hypocrisy, conflict, war. This will become as infuriating to
Westerners as it has been to Asians observing the same on the
part of the West. It may be that the things which divide Asian
countries will act as a brake on some national excesses in this
self-idealisation. It has been effective so far in the case of Japan's
war in Asia, for example, and presumably the Vietnamese will
continue to remind China that there are those who disagree
with the Chinese version of China's relations with the peoples
to its south. But myth-making is an important part of cultural
identity, and in an Asia-wide context there is now emerging a
mutually reinforcing process of myth-making, which is part of
the process of Asianisation itself.

In the end, because Asianisation is about international
politics and power, Asian values are about finding an alternative
way to that taken by the West and proposed by the West as
the way for all other societies. It may not yet have found a
unifying framework or construct. But because this is about the
search for an ideology to sustain resurgent Asian societies and
elites and a resurgent Asia, the search will go on irrespective
of whether the West challenges it or ignores it. And it will go
on because it is also about domestic politics and power within

Asian societies, and the domestic contest between 'traditional-ists' and 'democrats'.

ASIANISATION AND CONVERGENCE

Few in Asia have yet attempted to develop at length ideas for an Asian ideology, or a hypothetical or utopian 'converged' model or holistic identity for Asianisation, but many now see the need for a new organising framework of values and ideas to serve the next stage in global history. The inspiration or leadership for this is not seen as coming from the West, but as drawing on both Asian and Western values and traditions and beliefs; a convergence, but not in the way that most in the West might see it—a convergence onto a track more Asian than Western.

The lessons of history seem to suggest that superficial economic convergence does not necessarily lead to political or cultural convergence—in nineteenth-century Europe, for example, or in Europe's Asian colonies, or between Japan and the United States in present times. Examples of forced economic convergence, as in recent Europe, have even led to economic stagnation, inward-looking economies and, *together with other factors*, social alienation and decline.

What we have today between Asia and the West are simultaneous processes of convergence and divergence. Asian societies will continue to absorb such things as ways of governance and individual rights but at the same time try to resist and reject key aspects of Western influence, including such things as the adversarial dynamic, the erosion of family values, the breakdown of community, and unfettered individual freedom. The problem here is that economic modernisation does bring such problems, and Asian leaders are beginning to acknowledge that this is not an easy issue or one with a simple 'Asian' alternative.

Most proponents of Asianisation do not court divergence. But most suggest that convergence is something which has to be worked at by Asians, and that convergence onto the current condition of Western culture and the current expression of Western values is unacceptable, to many in the West as to many in Asia. A major difference between East and West is that the West, still being dominant, believes convergence can be left to work itself out, even if it contains destructive elements. The

East, not yet being dominant, wants to work at convergence. If Asian societies can take on the challenge of finding some way forward which does not lead to outcomes which are themselves lamented in the West, this is to be welcomed and should not be resisted.

One challenge for Asia is how to engage Western powers in the new scenario; in particular, how to engage the United States so that it becomes a stakeholder, has a vested interest in the new power equation, and sees it as an opportunity for its own renewal and not as a threat. Some Asian leaders have suggested that Asia might provide the leadership, and as the dominant force in regional and global politics offer an alternative way over a period in which an exhausted United States, which no one wants to expire, goes through its own regeneration. This is a long way from simple arguments about whether Asians value family more than Westerners do, and it puts the strands of Asianisation together into some kind of comprehensible whole.

There is a cautionary message for all who have an interest in this question. The voice of Asianisation is not an isolated voice, such as Dr Mahathir's for example, or the sometimes dismissively dubbed 'Singapore School', or the few others cited for what is often said in the West to be an unrepresentative idea. Thinking people in Asia are thinking about this issue, whatever word they may use to describe it, whatever the differences and variations in how they see it, and even if they do not openly express it to Westerners. It would be a mistake for thinking people in the West to imagine that this voice is anything other than an increasingly representative voice of Asia's influential elites.

EAST ASIA, ASIA-PACIFIC

Over the decade or so when all these ideas were forming in the minds of East Asians, Australia was focused on something completely different: the concept of Asia-Pacific. At the end of the 1980s it took a leading hand in the formalisation of this concept into APEC, the Asia-Pacific Economic Cooperation forum.

The semantic confusion and intellectual sloppiness in the Australian use of 'Asia-Pacific' to mean Asia, described in Chapter 1, has had important practical and policy ramifications. It has posed a conceptual problem for Australia, of which most

Australians are still unaware. Prime Minister John Howard, for example, at the end of his September 1996 visit to Indonesia, provided a recent example of this semantic and conceptual confusion between the two terms.[4] If we see Asia-Pacific and APEC, as we have, as representing Asia and as being the framework for delivering Asia to us and us to Asia, as we repeatedly implied, what do we think Asia actually is? Because APEC goes all the way to the Atlantic Ocean.

The distinction is not insignificant. If you travel constantly in Asia and talk with Asian elites, you are drawn into intellectual engagement every day with the subject of Asia and its future. It is something of a preoccupation among Asian leaders and opinion-makers. But most of what is discussed, except in close APEC circles, is about an Asia which has nothing to do with APEC. This is a different Asia. As early as the end of the 1980s this too was being talked of as having an institutionalised future as a regional community. So there was APEC and there was something else. The Australian Government and Australian officials dismissed and even derided this latter as being the idea of Dr Mahathir alone. This was an enormous and fateful judgment, because the something else also contained a different view of the way some people in the region looked at Australia. Within their concept of Asia, 'the region', or 'an Asian Community', often excluded Australia or was ambivalent about it. Some of the same people who welcomed Australia in APEC did not necessarily want Australia in an Asian Community. But because we thought Asia-Pacific = Asia, we did not listen, or said it was merely an attempt to compete with APEC, our APEC.

An illustration of the problem was a widely expressed Asian opinion after the March 1993 Australian election that Australia 'now' wanted to be part of Asia. The word 'now' glossed over the Australian role in APEC and gave it no credit in this, or for that matter in getting multilateral security in Asia onto the regional agenda. Australians were irritated. Were these Australian initiatives not about 'Asia'? The answer was no, not in this Asian perception. These long-standing Australian commitments were irrelevant to their concept of Asia. On the contrary, they were (and still are) cited as evidence that Australia hesitates at that leap of commitment which would make it what it claimed to want to be, part of Asia. And there was truth in this. For some Australians, at least, APEC was a very qualified way of committing to Asia. Such as, 'We'll go into Asia, but in the comfort of something that is not really Asia'. The old Western team! SEATO reborn! APEC is certainly still viewed in some quarters in Asia as having been set up as a vehicle for the United States, with Australia as a stalking horse.

So Australia by the 1990s was in a double difficulty. On the one hand it talked of Asia as the Asia-Pacific and saw its commitment to the Asia-Pacific as committing it to Asia, while on the Asian side people not only knew there was a difference between the two but were reserved about Australia being part of the former. This is what brought Australia to the point of its exclusion from ASEM in 1996.

In five or ten, or twenty or thirty years' time, there will be another framework within which all the countries of East Asia manage differences, deal with conflicts, handle economic and security relations, and begin the long process of accommodation of historical difference. This is in part what has given rise to Asianisation in Asia; it is where Asianisation will go next.

ASEM was a defining moment in the Asianisation of Asia. In many ways Australia had better credentials than most of the East Asians at ASEM—in terms of its general contribution to other countries in the region and its openness and tolerance, which are discussed in later chapters. But by our own stupidity, we were not there. Because in many important ways the concept of an East Asia *is* wide open, and doesn't belong to anyone. And that is why, even when governments of the region sense that there is now urgency in talking together about closer association, there is both reservation and intensity of manoeuvring among them, to try to ensure that no one else's national ambitions, no one else's philosophy, or culture, or language, or institutions, emerge as dominant in setting the directions. With diversity on almost every count, there are no ready-to-hand rules to define who should be in and who should be out. But there are three broad imperatives, on which Australia missed out, two by its own default, and the third resulting from the attitude of Malaysia. The first is that the participants must really want to belong. In the beginning in Europe, for example, there was the Common Market and the European Free Trade Association (EFTA), and they had different philosophies. Some really wanted to belong to the Common Market and some really wanted to belong to EFTA (and Britain didn't really want to belong to either). In Asia, Australia at first did not want to belong and then made a commitment which is highly qualified, in part by its hankering after the old relationship with the United States. The second is that each participating country must see its fundamental interests as being realised, even if over differing time-scales, primarily in and through that community. Australia did not see its fundamental interests this way. A third is that the originating participants must have some broad sense of which countries will constitute the core of the participation. This is what happened before ASEM, and because of our attitude on the first two counts, we were not there and had no say.

CHAPTER 4

A honey-coloured society?

Like all societies, Australia's is one of paradox and contradiction. In pluralist, democratic and individualistic societies in particular, of which the English-speaking Western democracies are the prime example, these paradoxes and contradictions are an essential part of the way in which society works, as for example in the concept of political opposition. There are always opposites, conflicting trends, exceptions, changes of course, two sides to the same picture.

The recent history of Australia's coming to terms with Asia is one of major paradox and contradiction. This is not surprising, because coming to terms with Asia is so confronting to the Australian identity. Australia had, after all, taken a very long time to come to an identity as Australian rather than something more derivative, and there are still many in Australia for whom even this process is not entirely comfortable, and many also for whom it has barely begun. At this point in our history, for Australians now to have to reconcile this identity with a future in Asia is challenge of a breadth and complexity little understood in Asia. It is not a matter of simple decision. Just to turn and face Asia full on required an enormous wrench for a society with our history.

These paradoxes are perhaps more apparent when we look back at the quarter-century since Whitlam was elected on 2

December 1972 and declared to a startled group of officials from Foreign Affairs in his office two days later that our 'neighbours', politically speaking, were now the Third World. After Whitlam we seemed to move forward and then back. We were enthusiastic but held back from total commitment. We had Whitlam's vision and then a decade of no vision. Consensus seemed to form and then break open. We made a choice about an Asian future and then declared it was no choice. We seemed to be for Asia, but then deflected that to an Asia-Pacific which embraced North America. We came to Asia but we did not make the hard intellectual engagement.

We therefore sent contradictory and confusing signals. This is of course due in part to lack of clarity and firmness in the thinking and articulation of Australian leaders. But in fairness it must also be understood that our adjustment to Asia *is* full of contradiction. As suggested in Chapter 1, there are two sides to the picture and one is cause for concern and even pessimism. The other is more optimistic and allows even an idealistic projection of our future. This is the base, the material on which we have to build. It is the corrective to that view in Asia which sees only the negative, and to the darker forces in our own society periodically exposed by bigotry and the failure in leadership exemplified in the latter months of 1996.

The greatest paradox and contradiction of the Australia of Asia forays and enthusiasms from the late 1970s to the mid-1990s was that, lazy about Asia intellecually, Australian *society* was actually starting to adapt to its Asian habitat, even if in a reactive kind of way. This paradox had something to do with that characteristic of Australia which is criticised in Asia as one of its great weaknesses, but which is also one of its great strengths: its laid-back nature, which of course also happens to be an important ingredient in its openness, receptivity and tolerance. Australia was changing also in ways unrelated to Asia over these two decades, and by the mid- to late 1980s there was a society which was not only lively, inventive and creative, but also culturally and socially cosmopolitan—and hard-working. We talk of an emerging new Asia. There has also been an emerging new Australia, whose Asia credentials are in some respects potentially, and paradoxically, as strong as those of many others to our north. This is the Australia I have argued in East Asia and sought to project in the region through the Asia–Australia Institute.

But many influential East Asians, who do not know or

perhaps like Australians, do not understand what has happened to this society, and find it difficult to believe that it can have changed. The proposition that Australian society is starting to shift its horizons and may be welcoming to Asian influence and even at ease with the idea of a future with Asia is to many East Asians compromised by what they see as a commitment which is highly conditional and far from sincere.

We must also remember that we have an unedifying past in Asia, whose imprint remains in the minds of many among the region's political and business leaders. Australia was something of a freak, a Europe-derived culture in a sea of Asian cultures, ruled by a transplanted European people soaking up sun and skin cancer in a climate for which they were never intended. Australia was also a client state, but it strutted in Asia with the airs often attaching to such clients, patronising and condescending to Asians and discriminating against them racially through the attitudes of individuals and the White Australia policy, under the protective wing of great and powerful friends. Many Asians who studied in Australia experienced at first hand the patronising of this earlier Australia.

It must be difficult to forget the brash Australian trailing around Asia with the pretensions of a global power, telling Asians what to do and how to behave, which I witnessed at first hand and with horror when I first went to live in Asia in 1962. It must be difficult also to forget the paternalistic atmosphere for Asian students in Australia. And given Australia's introduction to independent Asia as the client of the United States, it must be difficult not to be cynical about Australia's claims today that it is not still a mouthpiece for US interests in the region. Many of the people I talk to in East Asia see their own countries as having moved so far from where they were when they first knew Australia, and so fast, that Australia is seen as out of step, out of tune, and out of time. They see Australia as not having kept pace with what has happened to the region, unwilling to change, not contemporary in its performance or its attitudes.

There has been truth in that proposition. While in Asia I argue the evidence for a changing Australia, at home I remain a critic of our slowness to change. I have been one of those berating Australians for laziness in coming to terms with the fact of Asia, standing on the proselytising platform, urging that we go forward, lift our sights, change our cultural norms, accept Asia into our intellectual universe, find a place in the great group force which is driving East Asian societies forward in an excitement of mutual discovery. At the Asia–Australia Institute we run courses intended to change the intellectual and cultural horizons of senior executives and managers—social engineering for Asia, which we call 'remedial training for elites'. So I'm not soft on Australia, and I don't intend to be in case, when things seem to change a little, instead of pointing outwards to Asia we go back to lying on the beach, nose pointed upwards to the sky.

But we also have to remember where Australia is coming from to understand why change has been slow and difficult. For a broad cross-section of the Australian population, life in the early years after World War II was good. It was even too easy. There was a tiny population in a resource-rich continent. The sun came up and things grew. Even if you went to the beach they still grew. This didn't require economic management or reform, or gruelling sacrifice. We barely had to negotiate our export business. And when what should have been a terrible shock to the economic system happened—the beginnings of Europe and Britain's decision to go with it—Australia discovered that it had coal and minerals and metals which simply had to be tipped into the waiting carriers from the northern hemisphere, almost without negotiation or need for self-discipline or economic reform.

Life was so good that Australians could not only be self-indulgent, they could afford it. They could afford an often self-indulgent welfare system. They could afford to indulge business, which developed a kind of welfare mentality of its own, looking to government support and subsidy. They could even afford, government and business alike, to indulge unions to a point which sometimes went well beyond what was either equitable in economic benefits or necessary in terms of the capacity this gave unions to hold employers and sometimes the whole economy to ransom. There is nothing wrong with any of this—if you can afford it.

This earlier Australia also contained, and bred, objectionable attitudes towards the outside world. Australia was supremely Britannia-centric. Just as the sun shone, so also did Britain, and so also many of the objectionable views which Britain had in the nineteenth century on race and cultural superiority. Even the world of ideas itself was so dominated. The influence of nineteenth-century British perspectives persisted so strongly into twentieth-century Australian education that even the world of Australia did not exist in this intellectual universe, let alone Asia.

As long as most of Asia itself remained in colonial servitude or impoverished underdevelopment, or both, Australia could remain locked in these attitudes without feeling the slightest need to examine them. To Australians, life was good, and you didn't need to change. And if you didn't need to change, you had no change to manage and therefore you didn't need the strategic and long-term thinking for management of change, or the national capacities and attitudes to go with it.

It was hard to bring about rapid change in such a society. But the problem for Australia was that the world around it changed and the good life came to an end, but it had neither the habit of setting long-term objectives nor the jolting, wrenching, desperation of a national trauma to drive reform. There was no invasion or civil war or revolution to leave a country wasted and exhausted to the point where the only thing was the terrible urgency to pick itself up and fight to rebuild. There was no incentive of the hungry. Unlike so many countries in Asia, there was no sudden independence and suddenly-on-your-own with a population to feed but a chronically underdeveloped economy. No humiliation of aid-dependence.

So Australians didn't even think there was anything seriously wrong until long after it had begun to go wrong. They didn't realise that the countries of Asia about which they had been so condescending had begun to catch up and go past them, and they remained locked in their Britain-centred unconcern for the richness and excitement of these societies in their immediate neighbourhood.

That Australia has now changed, decisively and for ever. It may still have a long way to go before we can secure our future, but if proof of change is needed it is to be found in public attitudes in the last term of the Keating Labor Government and the first year of the Howard Coalition Government. In the March 1993 election, the Keating Government's policy statements on Asia gave a primacy to Asia in our foreign relations that went far beyond anything that had ever previously been contemplated, and allocated $60 million for special initiatives to lock non-government sectors into the government commitment. There was no opposition. In mid-year Keating visited Washington and told the United States to go easy on bargaining trade for social and political change in Indonesia and China, and later in the year he and other Australian ministers publicly took sides with Asian nations—Japan and China—against US positions which the US Government regarded as fundamental positions of principle in its foreign policy. This occasioned domestic comment, but still no opposition. Then, in December 1993, the government announced a new defence policy which dramatically shifted our primary defence relationships away from the United States and into enmeshment with our immediate Asian neighbours. There was no alarm.

On the domestic front, in February 1994 the Prime Minister and the State Premiers, meeting as the Council of Australian Governments (COAG) in Hobart, jointly adopted a report which recommended that Asian (but not European) languages become mandatory in Australian schools,[5] and in the same month the Minister for Defence announced that an Asian language would henceforth be a requirement for officers in the Australian defence forces. In the same month also—the tenth anniversary of the polemic against Asian immigration launched by historian Geoffrey Blainey—columnists and academic specialists from around Australia, invited to examine the theories and predictions of that polemic, found them to have been proved wrong by subsequent events, and the anti-Asian advocacy to have been largely rejected by the Australian people.

As the March 1996 election approached, the Labor Government attempted to scare the electorate with warnings that the Coalition if elected would not be accepted in Asia and that this would compromise our future. Although no political analyst remarked it at the time, this was an extraordinary commentary on the public attitudes of the day. Thirty years earlier, no party would have dared to make an election issue of a commitment to an Asian future for Australia. But in 1996, while there was public slanging on this matter between the contending parties, it was slanging about which side had the better Asia credentials and was more strongly committed to Asia. The public simply looked on in bemusement. When elected, the Coalition immediately set out to prove the Labor Party wrong, with an intensive round of visits by Foreign Minister Downer covering most of East Asia, and Deputy Prime Minister Fischer and other ministers also tracking back and forth across the region.

There are in their public positions indications of deep reservation about Asia, and even about race, in the ranks and in the heart of the Coalition Government, and a nostalgia for an international order long gone. But the economic imperatives which chain us to Asia were to them inescapable, as also were the domestic imperatives of a changed Australian society. Whatever sentiments may exist privately in this government, it has been out selling to Australian opinion-makers and the Australian public its credentials for handling relations with Asia, because it perceives that the society wants that assurance. This reflects an amazing change.

Politicians are of course not always right. But there seems to be near unanimity among them in this reading of how Australia has changed. Even those who dissent, for example from the non-discriminatory immigration policy, do so on the basis of extreme positions which in themselves confirm that the extremist now feels threatened. The dissenters who stood for office at the 1996 election simply proved the rule. At the 1949 election they would have had overwhelming support. At the 1966 election they would still have had a majority. In 1996 they numbered no more than three, and the one who was a member of the Liberal Party was disendorsed for espousing such views. Vigilance and firm leadership are of course always necessary on these issues, but firm leadership now would lay them to rest as it has done in the past.

This is all good news, but the problem remains that for Australia's leaders Asia is less a commitment of rational persuasion and more one of faith. For most people in positions of leadership in public and corporate life, you believed in Asia or you didn't. If we had looked at it analytically and objectively, intellectualising, and without cultural or psychological avoidance, at Asia as fact, we might have done 30 years ago what we are trying to do today. We might have done it in the 1960s when Britain made its decision for Europe. We might have done it in the 1970s when the economic rise of Asia became inescapable. In 1976 we sent a formal dispatch from the Embassy in Beijing forecasting that China would become the dominant economic force in this region before the turn of the century. In the formal response to that dispatch, the combined forces of all the major departments in Canberra involved in our foreign policy were mobilised to heap derision on that forecast.

But if the change of heart we now have is still neither thinking nor long-term, the societal change is nevertheless long-term, and profound. The seeds of this change go a long way back, to the first encounters with Asia of a different kind of Australian, a quiet Australian. Unlike the pretend colonialist or the Ugly Australian—the minority who provided journalists with slick headlines: the mug lair on the beach at Bali; the overt racist; the sex tourist; the middle-class backpacker exploiting the hospitality of impoverished Asian peasants—this Australian was never in the news, and this Australian was a regionalist of sorts, contributing directly to the region's future. Since the early 1950s such people, professional Australians, have been living and working, quietly and unobtrusively, in every country of the region with the exception of Japan, in significant but untrumpeted programs of technical cooperation. Australian engineers, technologists, scientists, teachers, health and medical specialists and other professional and technical people, all involved in a modest way in the development of the region. This was not about power. It was about helping people. No other country in the region has such a record, and with the recent exception of the aid programs of Japan, there is still no other Asian country which has such region-wide commitment.

There were others. A few academics had become deeply immersed in Southeast Asia. At the initiative of one of these, Jamie Mackie, a small group of intellectuals in 1959 created the Immigration Reform Movement, which began the process of dismantling White Australia. As Nancy Viviani remarks in her commentary on this movement, these people were not only trying to put an end to something they regarded as morally wrong, they were also about trying to 're-create' Australian society.[6]

There was also a small but growing number among the ranks of Australian diplomats who were quietly concerned. No one has yet written a history of the culture of our foreign service. When I first joined it, at the beginning of 1961, I found a culture which often seemed to style itself on the British Foreign Service, and many individuals who strove to present themselves as British, even down to their accents. Many of these people even had little knowledge of Australian society or culture. This persisted in some individuals for many years, and long after I had departed the foreign service for the second time in 1976, in the early 1980s I found myself in a meeting in China at which an Australian diplomat was explaining to some Chinese officials that Australia had not produced much in the arts before the 1970s and had nothing to speak of in feature films until quite recently (thereby sweeping away the path-breaking role of Australian film-makers in the first development of feature films). But by the 1960s there were Australian diplomats who were themselves of a different breed and a different cast of mind. A few, not many, learnt Asian languages. They were quietly concerned about their own society, in relation to what they found in their sojourns in Asia.

With the exception of the Immigration Reform Movement, these people—engineers and other professionals, teachers, academics, diplomats—did not organise for change and seldom agitated for it publicly. But they were a leaven in society.

The campaign against the Vietnam War was more stridently influential. The war divided Australian society, but it opened the way for change. We had fought in Asian wars before, but now half the Australian population did not agree. So something within Australian society was changing in relation to the region, and this change was attested with the election of Whitlam in 1972. As suggested earlier, Whitlam did not radicalise the Australian middle class, he Australianised it.

A small part of what Australianisation is about is Asianisation. This is an important distinction. Australia's Asianisation, in the sense in which I use it, is just one part of the coming to terms with the history, geography, habitat and future of Australian society. It does not mean abandonment of what is Australian. On the contrary, it means, or should mean, the strongest possible affirmation of an Australian Australia as the political culture within which Asianisation in our society can take place. I think it is no coincidence that people who are deeply committed to Australia coming to terms with Asia often have a passion for some aspect of European life or culture. Patrick FitzGerald was an example. Gough Whitlam is another. So also Paul Keating. This is not a contradiction; it is a balance and a harmony, and distinctively Australian.

Asianisation in Australia did not follow immediately on the 1972 election. It gathered force slowly. It was given a great push by the watershed decision of the Fraser Government in the late 1970s to admit large numbers of boat people from Vietnam (an act of leadership which must not be forgotten, dramatically confirming that the White Australia policy was not only ended but reversed), and brought Australia in the mid-1990s to a situation which most Australians would not have found acceptable at the end of 1972.

The Asianisation of Australian society is still in train, and it is driven by change on two fronts. One is Australia's external orientation, and the overwhelming concentration of our multilateral connections and networks with other countries of the Asian region. Two-thirds of our trade is now with Asia. China will soon replace the United States as our second largest export market after Japan, and Korea will also displace the United States by the turn of the century. Our trade with ASEAN is greater than our trade with the European Union. Asia also accounts for 40 per cent of our immigrants, and 50 per cent of net immigration (permanent departures over permanent arrivals). Forty per cent of inbound tourists come from Asia. More than 40 per cent of our tourists go to Asian destinations. Transport and communications, which tend to follow, not create, the pattern of a country's international relations, tell the same story. Nearly 50 per cent of the countries of origin and destination of the airlines operating into Australia are in Asia; 50 per cent of QANTAS outward passenger loadings are to Asia.

The whole fabric of Australia's external connections has shifted. In this sense, while Australia may not yet have committed itself or found complete acceptance in Asia, it belongs to no European or North American political or economic community. Its business people deal predominantly with Asian business people. Paul Keating's first overseas visits as prime minister were to Asia; John Howard as prime minister did the same. All this has reshaped the orientation of Australia and the influences on it. Think what it means in human terms. All of the 'knowns' in Australia's previous major relationships, with Britain and the United States and to some extent Europe, have had to be replaced with 'unknowns', in unfamiliar, Asian, cultures—unknowns in terms of connections, networks, local knowledge, the risk antennae you need to make decisions, the norms of personal behaviour. Trade is done by people. And numbers of Australians have actually proved very good at it in Asia. A seldom-noted fact is the significant number of Australians at the top in successful business in that most competitive of Asian cities, Hong Kong. But not just tall poppies. With two-thirds of our trade with Asia, think what this means for the people who drive trade: working together, locking horns, negotiating, tramping around factories, meeting in hotels, eating in restaurants, drinking in bars. They may not have learnt about Asia at school, but they are there now, and the influence on them is slowly changing Australian societal attitudes. In our external connections, then, we are part of Asia.

Together with this change in external orientation and connections, there is a second and greater change within Australian society itself. This is in what we apprehend, what we feel about it. There is in this a kind of Asia constituency in Australia, and for a time in the early 1990s, this idea of Australia being part of a wider regional habitat which is Asia was more in the attention, or perhaps more on the lips, of Australian politicians and business and other leaders than in any other country in the region. Leaving aside whether we have actually thought much about it, we are now, in this way at least, a good deal further down the track of commitment to Asianisation of our society than many others in the region—Japan, for example, or China. And even among the ASEAN states, which are approaching this question, few are yet taking on the challenge of a broader 'Asianisation' of their own societies. Given what this means for Australian society and the Australian political culture, this is quite a shock. It doesn't mean everyone in Australia is sitting around thinking 'We're going into Asia. That's terrific!', or even that most Australians would consciously support the proposition. But the degree of what might be called 'non-opposition' is a remarkable thing for a country with our political history. It will soon need a novelist to take us back to what Asia used to feel like and how we saw it in the abstract.

I know it is very easy to stir emotions of resentment and resistance to this process, but that is always possible on many issues—if you want to stir. But what strikes me as important is that Australia seems, without Australians or anyone else having noticed it much, to have passed something of a milestone in its political maturing. And I believe we can say that one thing that has changed decisively in Australia over the last decade is this feeling Australian elites have about Asia. 'That's the elites', you may say. 'What about the rest of Australia?' Is it true, as I am challenged every day when I travel in Asia, that Australian leaders may have made a commitment but that this is not shared by the Australian people? I'm not sure. They may not be committed supporters. But they seem less to be opposed, and this non-opposition is itself a fundamental change in the Australian political culture. And it became more pronounced in the late 1980s and early 1990s. Even on immigration. Where the emotional debate about Asian immigration in 1984 was seen as threatening to our Asia relations and even to our society, its subsequent surfacings have been progressively short-lived. I am worried by the possible effects of some policies and attitudes of the Coalition Government because they threaten to divide Australians in ways which could bring this issue into more sustained contention. But we do have in the Australian populace a degree of acceptance. A kind of Australian version of the Taoist virtue of being in a state of inaction, which in that philosophy is of course a positive and desirable state. It is desirable also in our society, and if it is stirred into action and opposition that will be a failing of leadership, not of the Australian populace at large.

If we think Asianisation in Australia is abstract or hypothetical, look at what else is happening. The shift in the Australian political culture draws on a concurrent shift in the Australian identity. If eating and sex are the two most basic activities of humankind, it can be observed that Australians are getting down to the Asian basics with a certain determination, one might even say gusto. In the history of Australian immigration in the 1950s, it will be remembered that migrants from Europe were regarded by the dominant English and Celts with suspicion, on many counts and particularly for their language and their food. Immigrant children were mocked in the playground, and even attacked physically, because of the strange food they brought to eat at lunch time. Every Australian now eats Asian food, frequently. And this is not just what is bought at restaurants or take-aways, in which Asian accounts for over 50 per cent. Asian elements are common in Australian family cooking. The average Australian family cooks some form of Asian 'stir-fry' at least twice a week. This is not whimsical indulgence of my own interest in Asian food. Food is a fundamental part of cultural acceptance. It has also been enormously important in moving Australia from its monoculturalism towards a richer identity. Not multiculturalism, which is only a process, but a singular Australian identity, with an Asian flavour.

Look elsewhere. It seems that we may be approaching sex with similar enthusiasm. Figures produced by the Australian demographer Charles Price show the rates of ingroup marriage among second-generation immigrant communities, which of course also indicate the rate at which people are marrying out of their communities, or out-marriage. They show that the rates of out-marriage in second-generation Asian immigrant communities are remarkably high, in the case of Chinese, 78 per cent, in the case of Indians, 96 per cent.[7]

That greatest of Australian success stories, Asian immigration, is surely one of the wonders of the modern world. Into this very small population, with all its history of racial exclusion, and its closed-shop attitudes in governments and universities and business corporations just as much as in the unions, where for reasons of labour market protection it was always strong, we have taken every year since 1978 a minimum of one-third of our immigrants from Asia—without major incident. A city like Sydney is in this respect almost more international than any other in Asia, the obviously European now interlarded with the Asian. A single graffito, a mad extremist in Perth, someone deported for reasons of bureaucratic bungling or stupidity, a bigoted politician on talk-back radio taken out of context, will get a big headline in an Asian newspaper, but the extraordinary achievements of our immigration policy seldom do. Asian features are appearing in Australian art and music and theatre and literature as well as in cuisine and physiognomy. And this immigrant body also enlarges the mesh of business and financial connections with Asia, making for a more cosmopolitan Australian business environment, which offers variety, choice, and difference.

Take education. You can't have an internationalist outlook if you leave it to others to be international and yourself remain dependent on them. Australian education could even be about to enter a revolution in this regard. The recent government acceptance of the need for Asian languages and the study of Asian societies in mainstream humanities and social science subjects in every school and in many primary schools by the early part of the next decade has a potential for Asianisation of an order which no other government in the region has yet contemplated. What this would do to the outlook of people entering the Australian workforce—if government funding follows government acceptance—is not simply beneficial to Australia's foreign relations. It would transform the intellectual universe of Australia's education systems, and the students who study in them and the teachers who teach in them and the parents of the students they serve. This is not yet fact. But it is a major step forward in recognition.

Across the spectrum of Australian life, there are a thousand other examples of the Asianisation of Australia in the two senses in which I use the term, of interconnectedness with Asia in our external relations and in our daily lives, and of bringing Asia into our social and cultural landscape.

Within this environment of social change, there have of course been immense changes also brought by the economic reform of our society—in financial deregulation, corporatisation and privatisation of government business enterprises, tariff reform and labour market reform. There has been substantial progress which is slowly putting an end to many of the self-indulgences of the past. This is a quiet revolution, undertaken by quiet Australians. It has not produced dramatic turns, because each move forward has been slow and sometimes painful. The dramatic effect will come progressively over the next few years, when the decision-makers in Asian countries find, each time they look at the Australian economy, that almost without noticing it, Australia has begun to move in step economically with its neighbours. The difficulty and apparent slowness of economic reform asks some understanding and patience from Asia, rather than the dismissive criticism I still sometimes hear. Australia perhaps has some right to ask for that understanding and patience. The tradition of the quiet Australian goes back a long way. They were understanding and patient when Asian countries were wrestling with the problems of development before they became economies of dynamic growth. Quiet Australians developed the Colombo Plan. Australia has been quietly helpful in many spheres, from defence to the development of schools and universities, and in the training of vast numbers of Asian people in commerce and economics and business and marketing and other less obvious but business-related disciplines, who have gone back to their Asian countries and become agents of the dynamic which is making Asian economies the focus of the global economy.

Unlike Europe and North America, which have opened their institutions to foreign students, Australia's commitment has always been first and pre-eminently to students from Asia. The result in Asia may not be as obvious as that of the education provided by the United States because of the size and weight of US resources. But the point is not about comparative visibility. It's about Australian credentials, and in this respect I think Australia can be, not a follower, but a leader in Asia. It is for this reason, incidentally, that I am not concerned about the brain drain out of some Asian countries into Australia. If we are to be a Community, there will always be such movement and settlement of professionals. It is of course greatly beneficial and enriching to Australia, and will help it to overcome some of the problems it has had in the past in coming to terms with its geographical milieu. But for Australia, it has always been a two-way process, since the 1950s. The accounting and legal professions in one or two places in Asia that now feel the pressure of brain drain have in fact been almost entirely populated over the years by graduates of Australian universities.

The education and training programs have also been an

ingredient in the tolerance with which the large flow of Asian immigrants since 1978 has been received. As in all countries of immigration, resentment stirs with concerns about employment and education and housing. You can always get negative views from opinion polls if you ask the right question, and failure in leadership will allow these views to fester in public. But qualitative research has shown that there is also a high degree of tolerance and acceptance, including in working-class areas of high Asian migrant concentration. Many middle-class families now have some relative who has lived in an Asian country. Many middle and working-class houses have been home to students from Asian countries. Many process workers now find that the next person on the line is from an Asian country, that the next-door neighbour is Asian.

I suppose we could add 'many Australians have fought in Asian wars'. I have reservations about this because I don't agree with the Australian motivation in some of these wars. But if you look at Europe, the fact is that the enmeshment of the countries of Europe has been an enmeshment in war as well as in peace. Australia has something of that experience, although if we ask the question 'at whose behest?' it leaves open the answer to how much wisdom about Asia we acquired from these experiences. But there is something to be observed from Australia's involvement in Asian wars. The fact that every occasion, beginning with our belated part in quelling the Boxer Rebellion in China at the turn of the century and arriving at Vietnam, was always at someone else's behest and in latter years against strong domestic opposition illustrates the point that Australia itself has had no traditional fights with any part of the region.

This puts it in an interesting position in relation to an Asian Community. Situated at the southern end of this Community, it might sometimes seem, geographically and politically, to be at the margin. But the fact that it has no history in war or in intimate friendship or cultural or ethnic consanguinity like that which so complicates the relations of China and Japan, or Indo-China, or Singapore and its neighbours, makes it in a way equidistant from each one of the countries of the region. It is both equidistant and intent on closing the distance. And that is a potentially useful position, both for Australia and for the rest of the region.

This is where Australia has now arrived. Externally, largely by luck or default or someone else's initiative. Domestically, by a long and sometimes difficult process of social change. But here we confront the two sides to Australia, and the question of whether we are prepared to apply ourselves intellectually to the next 30 years. The positive side is encouraging. In terms of parliamentary democracy, and the rule of law, and the basic freedoms, and equality, and the liberalism and humanism of our democratic tradition, Australia has the most open and tolerant society in the region. We may not be top of the class in understanding our neighbours, but we may be top in these other ways.

There are also of course many kinds of Australian: the crypto-Brit, aping the manners and accent of upper-class British civil servants; the servant of US interests, sliding around Asia in borrowed garb and protection; the uncultured 'colonial'; the unsophisticated and awkward and gauche, uncertain of how to behave, uncertain of their own identity, intimidated by people from older and more wily civilisations. But there is an Australian kind of Australian who is a nationalist, who has no feeling of shame about anything except that which is shameful, like the treatment of Australia's indigenous people; who has enjoyed the benefits of a sophisticated and liberal education; who has no cultural cringe and does not nod in servile assent when British or Chinese or Indonesians say Australia has no culture, but who rejoices in a contemporary culture which is more vibrant than that of almost any other contemporary culture in the Asian region, and which flourishes without political constraint or interference. Whose country can produce great films, and Nobel prizewinner Patrick White, or Booker prizewinner Thomas Keneally, or world-renowned musicians; which sends ballet to acclaim in New York, orchestras to applause in Vienna; which each week sees publication of a dozen new novels, openings of painting exhibitions; which each day packs concert halls and theatres; which acclaims composers like Peter Sculthorpe whose music is infused with the musical traditions of Asia; which transplants hearts and livers and develops solar energy and lives by science and reason. This Australian is one who acknowledges the European cultural heritage and sees no reason to deny it, but who sees the Australian identity as the here and the now and not the there or the yesterday, and whose here and whose now is in an Asian setting. This is, if you like, the Australian Asian, which has nothing to do with race.

This is the kind of Australian we will see increasingly in the region. In the corridors of Canberra, smart young bureau-

crats see power and career in things to do with Asia. These are
the people we will see at regional meetings, and in the next
decade more of them will be speaking Asian languages. Australian academics, jumping on and off planes in Asian capitals,
begin to see their country's future as Asian. Catholic schools,
research institutes, State governments, film-makers, architects,
tour operators, journalists and producers of salmon, lobster,
asparagus, avionics and heart pacemakers are absorbed with
the issue of how to become involved in Asia. The Australianisation of Australia now has this inseparable Asian dimension.

It doesn't mean all Australians will become 'Asian' in
ethnic or physiognomical terms. But this is one other respect
in which Australia could turn out to be uniquely part of this
region. If race were to be one thing which identified what is
Asia, then with immigration and intermarriage, and the prospect this brings of a honey-coloured society (honey ranging as
it does all the way from white to black), the heritage of the
Australian Australian will be an enriching blend of European
and Asian, a cosmopolitan truly fitted to be a member of an
Asian regional community.

That kind of Australia is part present, part future, and it is still
hovering between the contradictory sides of its nature. But the
lucky country of which Donald Horne wrote 30 years ago is
unfortunately not only no longer lucky, its future is no longer
even assured. ASEM was a first ominous warning of that. Even
if we succeed in joining ASEM, the ASEM process illustrates
that the votes which will determine our future are not in
Australia but in Asia, and they will not necessarily go our way.
As Anne Kent has written in relation to China, when we had
the Cold War and the United States had China pinned against
the wall, we had great freedom to initiate and pursue relatively
independent China policies.[8] Now that there is no Cold War
and China is feeling its strength in Asia, our China policy is
determined by what China itself does. The same applies increasingly to all of our relations with East Asia.

So even if we have a measure of adaptation to Asia in our
society, this does not yet deliver our future. We face a future of
a kind we have never experienced, have not thought about and
do not know how to manage. This is a future in which societies
with which we have no traditional networks or cultural or
linguistic affiliation will determine what happens to us internationally and domestically. We are doubly disadvantaged by

the fact that every one of these other countries in East Asia has had this kind of experience, has thought about it, has had to manage it, and tends to think long-term. We should not be fatalistic about this, but unless we do turn our minds to this question, and the long term, and the preservation of our society, we will lose Australian democracy and become a supplicant state. This makes education, and what we do with it from now on, crucial to the survival of our social system.

CHAPTER 5

Asia, education and the Australian mind

What is needed from our education? It is not just training in certain skills or even adding Asia to the existing curriculum. It is an opening and refurnishing of the Australian mind.

Until quite recently, the whole of our education from kindergarten to the end of university assumed that there was but one world of learning, one universe of intellectual activity and contribution to humankind, and that was the world of Europe and its derivatives (including the United States), which was the world of education in Britain when it was transplanted to Australia in the nineteenth century. As late as the early 1990s, more than 95 per cent of Australian children still got all the way through education to the end of university without learning anything about Asia in their formal education. This situation is improving slightly, but while there are no statistics, the optional status of most Asia subjects makes it likely that more than 80 per cent remain untouched by serious study of Asia. This is not in Asian languages, where the percentage is much worse, but in anything at all: in history and geography and literature; in religion and philosophy; in music and painting and theatre; in the history or contemporary state of science, medicine or mathematics. The contributions of non-Europeans, where they are mentioned, are still largely eccentricities.

This kind of education produces an Australian who is

ignorant of Asian societies and has no cultural or intellectual orientation towards them. It produces relationships with Asia in which the Asian party must do all the work. They learn our language; we do not learn theirs. In their schools and universities they may not learn about each other but they do learn about the kind of society and culture from which we have sprung; we do not have the same knowledge in respect of their countries. They are able to walk in step with us; we are unable to walk in step with them.

When you consider this absence of half the universe from the central content of Australian education, you have to wonder. Is it a careless, 'lucky country' unconcern with what's out there? Is it a conscious shutting of the minds of Australian educators, feeling exposed and insecure, remote from their cultural and educational inspiration? Is it the auto-culture of the many cultures in Australia—my culture first and be damned to all the rest? Or a sheltering of young minds against the threatening East, White Australia living still in the Australian classroom?

Whatever the explanation, you can't escape the impressive lack of intellectual curiosity in this exclusion from the core of Australian education of the several worlds which lie between the Persian Gulf and the coast of California. You can't help wondering about the philosophers of Australian education, and the pedagogues in our universities and schools, and those who dispense money to education, or withhold it.

And you can't help wondering about those who set the agenda on these things. It's not as though Asian societies, in some sense at least, haven't been on someone's education agenda in this country. As long ago as 1964, Paul Hasluck spoke at the Australian College of Education on the subject of Australia and its neighbours.[9] So over 30 years ago the issue was on the agenda of that college. These 30-odd years have seen a generation of educators go by, while those involved in promoting the study of Asian languages and societies in Australia have seen several false dawns. It is true that Australian education stirred itself in the mid-1960s and, under the impetus of the Auchmuty Report in 1970,[10] increased the pace, but the movement slackened in the mid-1970s and nearly died in the 1980s as part of the malaise of the mind in that decade.

Why that happened is a very interesting question. It is obviously not enough just to debate the issues or set an agenda. An agenda, after all, is merely a list of things to do, the business of the day. What is in question is more like a matter of belief. Why do we not talk of setting an education *philosophy* for the next several decades? Then we would have to focus on the intellect rather than merely drawing up strategies and programs—the common stuff of agendas. I wonder if we are not afraid of using our intellects in this way, if we are not scarred by the profound and painful debates of the past on those sensitive matters of belief about what it means to be an Australian. Or are we still just squeamishly fearful of lowest common denominator anti-intellectualism?

For we cannot escape the fact that in the matter of bringing Asia into *mainstream* Australian education—and hence into the Australian mind—there are philosophical issues that have to do not just with change, which is always challenging, but with the whole cultural and intellectual orientation of Australia. To raise the question of the study of Asia was clearly not enough. Where we, the Asia specialists and scholars in Australian education, failed was in not taking on the philosophical issues and pushing them to the very limits of debate. And we failed also to grasp that change in education has to do with power, in these ways: with the power of an idea, with who wields power in our institutions, and with the power of the vocabulary in which education is debated.

Paul Hasluck said some interesting things to the Australian College of Education in his 1964 Buntine Oration:

> One of Australia's problems is that a more and more self-centred western Europe is leaving China and South-East Asia to someone else—or to chance.
>
> We have to rely on our intelligence rather than on our strength.
>
> We have certain possible advantages as a European country in this region of being able to be heard in two places at once and of possibly being able to see situations in the round.
>
> The economic future of Australia will become increasingly involved in the economic future of the region.

The last three of these comments could be contemporary. But it was the philosophy behind them that was the problem, and the first quote gives it away. This is the idea that China and Southeast Asia could not be left to themselves but to 'someone else', or to 'chance', the latter suggesting paternalistically that if someone else was not in charge there could only be chance—not Chinese or Southeast Asians. Where are the people in this view? The Australian government of the day was desperately afraid that the United States might lose its resolve to remain militarily involved in Asia in the confrontation with Asian communism, and Hasluck was both architect and expositor of an Australian policy to strengthen that resolve.

Hasluck's beliefs were part of the fears of his time, the anxiety caused by the prospect of being left alone in an alien world. They were not such as would have made Australians consider the philosophical and intellectual implications of this situation, or make it the basis of a new impulse in Australian education. His interest in Asia sprang from concerns which saw Asia as essentially external to us, even if he saw these concerns as being about our survival. His interest in the economic potential of Asia was one which posed no challenge to our intellectual universe. His world of Asia was not intimate to our being but a thing apart.

And that is how, for the most part, for the next twenty years, we went about the matter of the study of Asia—as a thing apart. What little we did was in a few subjects or departments of 'Asian Studies', which, when you think about the problems of definition of what constitutes Asia, were not much superior in conception, intellectual justification or pedagogical underpinning to the centres of orientalism in Britain and Europe which were their models. We did not bother too much about primary or high schools, of course, because something which is peripheral to intellectual and cultural life has no place in the central currents of school education. That is why the endeavour nearly died. It didn't force its way into the central issues of debate or matters of belief in education. It failed on all three counts in the matter of power. We lost a generation of opportunity.

The way in which that opportunity faded and re-emerged, in the late 1980s, is instructive. There was the brief flowering of interest in the early 1970s provoked by the Auchmuty Report. This interest, on the part of government, gave Australia the grand sum of $1.5 million and the famous Alfonso texts which became the foundation of much Japanese language teaching here and in the United States and Canada.[11]

But the initial enthusiasm waned, and because it was not Asia in all our studies but Asian Studies, it is not surprising that other concerns simply crowded Asian Studies out. Inflation, unemployment, declining school enrolments, comprehensivisation were among the preoccupations of education at the time. And because Asian Studies seemed in the mind of government and the public to be about coping with that something up there to our north, the end of the Vietnam War meant to many that we didn't have anything immediately to cope with. The arrival of multiculturalism intensified this internal preoccupation. The matter of the Australian identity was now an issue, but it wasn't about what distinguishes a peculiarly Australian society and what distinguishes this society from others and how this society can relate to an external milieu which is of different cultural origins. It was about what distinguishes one's identity from that of other people living in Australia. (See Chapter 8.)

The mid–1970s saw one other development. Partly out of dismay at the rise and fall of government interest in the study of Asia, the professional Asia scholars established the Asian Studies Association of Australia (ASAA). There were great internal differences over how 'political' this body ought to be in lobbying for the cause. But at the end of that decade it produced a detailed report,[12] the first time the profession had developed an extended case for the study of Asian languages and societies in Australian education. This was submitted to the government. Among other things, it recommended the establishment of an Asian Studies Council. Power was at last on the list of things to attend to.

It took six years and a change of government for this council to come into being, and the process was not easy. The idea of a council was considered and rejected by a large interdepartmental committee in Canberra. The problem then became how to attract the attention of the politicians, and the answer was found in that which preoccupied Australia most, the economy. The small committee set up to look afresh at the idea of a council was established within the Department of Trade, then headed by John Menadue under John Dawkins as minister, although it was a tripartite committee embracing also the departments of Education and Foreign Affairs. It was also chaired by a former head of the Department of Trade, Jim Scully. And when it came to the actual establishment of the council, there was even some discussion about which of the three ministers it ought to report to, before it was finally agreed, between John Dawkins, Bill Hayden as Minister for Foreign Affairs and Education Minister Susan Ryan, that it ought to be Education.

The selling of the idea was critically dependent on the arguments of economic dependence on the Asian region. The arguments were about doing better in Asia, selling more, making more money, and it was on these arguments that the recommendation sailed through Cabinet and secured financial support. The early statements of ministers and other politicians are couched overwhelmingly in these terms. If they did have other grounds on which they had accepted the need for the study of Asia, to sell the idea publicly ministers simply had to beat the economic drum. The same was true of the Asian Studies Council itself after its establishment in 1986, and I had many arguments with colleagues in the ASAA about the need to keep pushing this line in order to keep the government committed.

Significantly, while this was going on in the late 1980s, such words as 'future', 'destiny' and 'survival', and such expressions as 'part of' and 'belong to' were around, at least in the vocabulary of Australian debate about our relations with Asia if not in solid thinking about the future. The last two are of interest, because the emphasis on economic arguments did not quite mean that the sole or fundamental reason for Asia being in our education was the economic imperative of our geographic location. The idea of 'part of' or 'belong to' raises very different questions for education. If we could be part of the Asian region and still also part of Europe, did that not say something about what is part of what on this globe? And about what is the universe of human creativity and what therefore ought to be embraced within the world of learning for all students passing through schools and universities irrespective of where in the world they live? It is not a merely strategic or economic matter but one that touches our manner of living humanly on this earth.

The new Asian Studies Council was asked to prepare a strategy for the government. Now how can you have a strategy without a vision, without saying something about where you're going and why? This is a difficult proposition, which I had to confront as chairman of the Asian Studies Council and separately over roughly the same period in the area of immigration policy. When you are given a brief to produce a set of recommendations, a document on the basis of which government can act, and you're not really asked to define what you understand by Australian society, I suppose you can respond by producing an agenda. But that seems hardly sufficient, and the experience of government commitment to Asian Studies over the entire time since I first encountered Asia in the teaching of the great

George Wilson at the University of Tasmania in 1958 had been that without the underlying philosophy, the matters of belief, of knowing what kind of ideal you have for Australia beyond the classroom or the agenda, you get nowhere. The government asks for a strategy. You can't responsibly respond without giving them something which is really a statement about the nature of Australian society, about the Australian identity, about a vision for the future. And that, if you are honest about it, will always be subjective, but you hope it will be a contribution of sorts.

We wrestled over that document, *A National Strategy for the Study of Asia in Australia*,[13] and when the first draft went to government departments there were strong objections, not so much over the strategy as over the language and what that implied. Cabinet accepted that draft, which then became the basis for the funding of the many programs now in place, but it was to the language that some ministers objected. It was feared by some that the emotive issues of the immigration debate—then, in 1988, in the full flood which followed the report of the Immigration Committee of which I was also chairman[14]—would wash destructively into the implementation of the strategy for Asian Studies. To some extent that happened, but for other reasons.

But in the vocabulary of discussion, one of the seminal terms from that drafting process was taken up: 'Asia-literacy'. In Hasluck's 1964 Buntine Oration there was discussion of education for Asian students in Australia, but nowhere was there any comment on the need for Australians to learn the languages and study the cultures and societies of Asia. Hasluck's philosophy seemed to reflect a view that Australia possessed an 'advanced civilisation' and there was no apparent reason why we should have to understand Asia. But Asia, of course, would have to understand us. Asians have certainly attempted to do so, and with dramatic results. They speak our language, they have studied the scientific and economic ideas of the West, and are building on the ideas rapidly to increase the social and economic status of their societies.

The fact that the term 'Asia-literacy' passed into the vocabulary did not mean that Asia-literacy was fact or that it would inevitably become so. It is not an elegant term, but it was intended to be an unthreatening and accessible way of getting at the essential problem of the intellectual uses of the study of Asia and the question of the Australian identity, and it is central to what the Asian Studies Council was saying about the study of Asia. Between now and Asia-literacy there are formidable barriers.

It is not coincidental that the key word is literacy, not economics or trade. For the road to Asia-literacy lies, not wholly, but significantly, within the study of the humanities. The 1980 report of the American Commission on the Humanities had this to say:

> The humanities have no rigid institutional or intellectual boundaries. They occupy a central place in our national culture, they help shape the meaning of individuality and citizenship and they pose fundamental questions about the human purposes of science and technology.[15]

Such a definition allows for the inclusion of the social sciences, and science and technology, in their humane interpretation at least. And while we may not have the benefit of an Australian companion to *The Closing of the American Mind*,[16] if America could affirm the place of the humanities in education (having neglected it for decades), could we not do so too?

In the Annual Lecture of the Australian Academy of the Humanities in September 1989, John Hardy had the following to say:

> Australia at the threshold of the twenty first century must arguably be a player in its own region or a pauper in its own region and what should, I think, be recognised is that this country is uniquely placed to contribute to the ongoing process of defining its own region—which is not simply a matter of substituting Asian Studies for European Studies. I do not however underestimate the enormous challenge involved in helping to define our evolving region, but it is a challenge which can only be appropriately undertaken if the humanities accept and play their part in it.[17]

There might seem to be an echo of 1964 in this, and I would caution that we first have to find acceptance in our region before there is any chance that we will be a welcome participant in the process of defining it, and that, as ASEM showed us, we are not yet accepted in Asia as having demonstrated our will to belong, partly because of what we fail to do in the matter of speaking the languages and learning about the societies of that part of the world. But Hardy's message about the humanities should be taken to heart, because we have a problem.

Our problem is that we not only have to study the humanities with a new perspective but that we have to reintroduce the humanities into our schools. This is not to turn the clock back to some idealised golden age of education, but to admit that there has been a process of levelling in education, in which the sustained study of difficult subjects which are not immediately or obviously relevant has been played down and even ridiculed. It may be true that only some children will study large numbers of these subjects over long periods of time, but they ought to be encouraged. If comprehensive schools cannot cope with this then other institutions should be established which can. Such institutions could have extremely broad formal curricula, perhaps ten or twelve subjects at Year 11 and at least six at Year 12. Such structures are unremarkable elsewhere, in Germany, for example, or in China. Why can they not exist here?

A major reason for the decline in the humanities, embracing a set of very real problems, is one many are familiar with—the 'crowded curriculum'. Foreign language learning was one of the early and serious casualties of the crowded curriculum and the push against the humanities. Its re-establishment is being attempted in the face of the exclusion of foreign languages from the current idea of what ought to be part of the education of every child.

But within the rest of the humanities and the social sciences there is a possibly more complex problem: that within these subjects minority, faddish, political and ideological interests are addressed. Now many of these new subjects ought to be available, even some of those which are narrow and likely to be of ephemeral relevance. But they are included in the curriculum *at the expense of such subjects as History and Geography*. This has not simply been devastating for the humanities: it actually puts History and Geography at their level or below, and to equate these subjects to History and Geography seems to me to be intellectually grotesque. This is what I mean by the levelling in education.

With this kind of thinking (if thinking it is), and with the Social Education movement leading the humanities and the social sciences, and the rise of the process- and issue-based curriculum, and the devolution of decision-making in curriculum to school or classroom, we have, not crowded curriculum, but curriculum anarchy. In many systems the curriculum is so open-ended that it is impossible to find out what students learn or don't learn, know or don't know. But we cannot infinitely accommodate diversity of content where the choice is individual or capricious or makes no critical selection but gives all subjects an equal value. And how can we even know whether the study of Asia deserves a place in such a curriculum? We can only add it to the list of competing subjects, last among equals, and even then we still will not know if it is being taught, or whether what started out as a national imperative is in any way finding reflection in the classroom.

Of course, what I propose is selective. But all cultures are by definition selective, and with the exception of education, and the more doctrinaire propositions of multiculturalism which hold that all cultures are equally equal, so also is Australia. Yet in our education we seem intent on producing a society without the intellectual means to distinguish or decide between anything, and particularly between competing beliefs or standards. It is not surprising that our frameworks for discussion are agendas rather than matters of belief. How then can you have a philosophy within which to consider the place of Asia in education? There can be no philosophy in a society if it denies that there is a basis for questioning any assumptions and asserts that all assumptions, beliefs and practices are therefore equally valid.

The levelling-down process, which masquerades as equality, discriminates against excellence as it does against discriminating enquiry. Excellence carries the taint of 'elitism', and it seems that in some of our systems educators quite specifically do not want to produce elites. But elite is *not* a dirty word in Australia, except in some ideological circles. As has been pointed out time and again, excellence is the very essence of our approach to sport, and the same applies to entertainment and gambling of various types—the offerings of 'the good life'. The disturbing thing is that while we enlist 'elites' to bid for the elite prize of elite sporting competition, the Olympic Games, and in 1996 quarantine elite sport from savage budget cuts, we have never seen such strength of elite support for an elite intellectual, artistic or scientific endeavour, and the same 1996 budget reduced the funding of all of these latter fields. We have lauded the head-above-the-crowd attainments of the 'last tycoons' of the Australian business world; we barely know which Australian won the Nobel Prize for literature. What is applauded in the world of sport, entertainment, and financial risk-taking is disparaged and denied in the Australian Parliament and in the classroom. What kind of intellectual leadership can that provide to the next and future generations?

It is almost impossible to inject intellectual arguments about Asia into such a 'culture', and so we have the phenomenon of the immediately utilitarian. Look at the growth of Japanese in the 1980s. Other Asian languages and studies were barely visible.

So we have to change the culture. Because the challenge of the humanities is an intellectual challenge. It is about the proper study of mankind but also about what is humankind, about what is the proper intellectual universe of our education, about what is valued, what is excellent, what is beautiful, what is moving, what is lasting—about what are the matters of belief. Our matters of belief.

To go on excluding the non-European or non-Western from the mainstream of our education is intellectually and educationally and morally untenable. As creatures of this education we need to remind ourselves what it excludes.

1. The historical contribution to contemporary science, technology, mathematics and religion of these cultures, which is at least equal to that of the West. The ideas which gave birth to the computer, for example, have their ancestry in China. Our mathematics derives from the Arab world. Christianity itself is an 'Eastern' religion.

2. In philosophy and painting, in astronomy and geography, in architecture, sculpture and theatre, in hydraulic engineering, and literally dozens of other subjects, these cultures which lie in that *terra nullius* of Britannia-centric Australian education have contributed to the history and culture and civilisation of humankind in quality and quantity by no means inferior to that of Europe.

3. Some of these major and independent cultures have developed unbroken over the period since European antiquity. They are not dead but living. They represent more than half of the world's people. And they are reflected in living languages spoken, in many cases, by populations many times greater in number than linguistic groups in Europe whose numbers we regard as significant.

4. The contemporary politics of Asian states, even if we disregard the impact on our own society, are vital and sophisticated and complex and colourful. They may even be more instructive about the politics of Western states than the study of our own societies, because of the process by which they examine, dissect, convert and implant into their own

bodies politic aspects of government which have grown up in a Western democratic environment.

5. Their conduct of international relations and diplomacy, through history as well as in the international politics of today, while no more perfect in avoiding conflict than the West, has elements of delicacy and sensitivity and subtlety which we have lost, or simply never had.

6. If the discipline of economics is essentially Western in origin, the study of economics can be nowhere more rewarding than in the study of Asian economies in this twentieth century.

If we exclude all or most of this from the general education of our children what does it do? Is a general education which takes little or no account of this more than half of humankind justifiable as the legacy of learning we bequeath to those we teach? There is a twofold intellectual benefit in learning about Asian societies. The first is that if teaching about Asia raises awkward questions about ourselves and others (human rights might be one such), then it can advance our critical understanding. The second is that there is a world, or rather several worlds, of ideas we do not know, but which the study of Asia will open to us. So students stand to benefit intellectually. And an Australia-centric education, if modern, informed, enlightened, esteeming quality and pursuing excellence, and committed to the balanced intellectual development of our children, cannot be called such if it excludes from the learning entitlement of all children this intellectual benefit.

By an Australia-centric education I mean an education which joins the intellectual and cultural and historical wellsprings of Australia: European, Aboriginal, Asian, and something which is ultimately larger, and which we can unashamedly call 'Australian'. This is important, because to have such an education we have to have a strong sense of who we are. We have to be clear about the Australian identity, more than at any time in the past. A changing and uncertain world order, pressure from our neighbours as we move with them to form an Asian Community, internal debate about a republican future, multiculturalism's preoccupation with what divides us one from another instead of what we have in common, all these demand that we take up and assert our shared Australianness.

The problem is not just in the schools. The 1990 report *Priorities in Higher Education*[18] accurately identifies a problem of what it calls 'cultural illiterates—[those] ignorant of the literature, history, political science and sociology of the society in which they will practise their profession, and on which they, collectively, will have a profound influence'. The report on Asia in Australian higher education commissioned by the Asian Studies Council[19] also identified breathtaking deficiencies in tertiary Asian languages and studies and teacher education, which have only marginally been overcome.

By an Australia-centric education I do not mean tokenism, with bits of this and bits of that; or multiculturalism; or any 'ism' other than the pluralism which makes Australia an open and undogmatic society. What I mean is an integrated, structured, intellectually rigorous and discriminating curriculum which is identifiably and uniquely Australian, which both embraces the study of Australian society and reaches out to our regional and, beyond that, global environment, and which is formed within an idea embracing where we are in place and time and not by a world which no longer exists. Such an education will, of course, be concerned with much more than the study of Asia. But it is the proper context in which to develop such study. We do not want an 'Asianisation' of the curriculum so much as an Australian education in which Asia has a natural place.

The study of Asia has to find its place mainly in the humanities and social sciences, and if these are intellectually and institutionally weak, so also will be our capacity to cope with our immediate external environment. If we place high value on the humanities and social sciences, and value culture as 'hard', then the logic for including the study of Asia is much more apparent than if Asia is seen as an elective along a line of 'soft' options with no relevance to real life or employment, or which equates Asia with home science.

The idea that 'culture' is as critical to our future and our survival as science and economics would certainly not be widely accepted in Australian schools, but it is nevertheless the case. And as with the push for Asian languages, which found political support because of their utilitarian application, so also with the study of Asia we may have to use utilitarian arguments to grab the attention of politicians long enough to be able to put the rest of the case. The hard issues of today, hard in terms of both the centrality of the issue and the prospects for employment, include many which require that we educate people in these subjects which come within the broad definition of culture. The environment is one; human rights, an issue which, for example, has seriously undermined the economic relationship between the United States and China, is another.

But perhaps the most interesting concerns our economic relations with Asian countries. There is now much anecdotal evidence that where we have had poor economic performance in Asia it was a cultural problem rather than economic one. It seems to me that the problem is twofold. First, even within our own country, we seem to have lost the capacity to relate what we are trying to do economically to the base culture of Australia. If you look at what happens in the successful Asian economies, you see that their economists have studied at the same schools as ours, whether in the United States or Britain or Europe. But when they go back to their countries, they tend to graft this learning onto the base culture, drawing on its strengths, stepping round its weaknesses. We do not do this. And second, because we don't relate economics to our own culture, which we don't learn about much at school, and because we also don't know about Asian cultures, which we don't learn about at all at school, we have a very serious problem. These problems call not for micro-economic reform, but for micro-cultural reform. And that is very hard.

I understand that children do not study subjects because they are in the national interest, that they study them because they are interesting or challenging or give them a means of understanding the world or a path to employment. And I appreciate that making the study of Asia attractive to children as well as serving the national interest is an extremely difficult task. Our culture is increasingly heterogeneous, and a sense of national direction in education is still resisted by influential minority groups. Yet this generation of Australian children will be required to operate in national, regional and global contexts which were impossible for most Australians to imagine even a decade ago. The skills and knowledge they will need in 2020 must be in mainstream education today, or our society will stumble, and fall. The well-educated Australian must have both arts and science, in different mixes and at different levels, according to individual talents. But the total pool must reflect the union of a society which aspires in all respects to be excellent. Perhaps we should aim to be the 'excellent country'. I think we should.

The change we need, which cannot be put off for another 90 years, is that compelled by changing political, economic and social conditions internationally and within Australia, which will no longer allow us to continue without national direction in a way that may have been appropriate for a group of disparate colonies scattered across the continent in the latter part of the nineteenth century. If this process is handled sensitively, I see no reason for there not to be a continued devolution of power to schools of those matters which schools are best placed to decide, and that would include some elements of curriculum. Perhaps the need for large education bureaucracies might even decline!

Language learning is fundamental to education. It is true that English is a kind of lingua franca around the region and that you can get by with English. But getting by is hardly enough. It means that other people can have the means of reaching a very good understanding of you and your society, but that you do not have the same capacity in respect of them. English gives you one-way communication and a limited information flow, filtered through what other people or other sources make available to you and in whatever form they decide.

To illustrate how language affects business, for example, take the case of English brand names of Chinese products. I once had to talk to a Chinese state-owned corporation responsible for packaging and branding of Chinese consumer goods for export markets. There were some problems. Among Chinese toilet paper brands there were Double Happiness, Cat and Ball, As You Like It, and Thumbs Up. There was the Spring Thunder radio, Great Leap floor polish, Front Gate underpants, the White Elephant battery, Mouldy Biscuits, and Swine Chocolates (for the Middle East). I mention these not to laugh but to point up the language problem for us and the cultural problems relating to language. In Chinese, many of these names are very common brand names which appear on many products. There are also, for example, Double Happiness cigarettes. The name itself does not appear exceptional on either toilet paper or cigarettes in Chinese. But the marketing people had not concerned themselves with what happens when these are translated into a different language and a different cultural context. Double Happiness is a dubious proposition in Western countries when associated with smoking. Double Happiness toilet paper is open to a number of constructions, and Thumbs Up betrays a lack of consciousness of the connotations of that expression in English. The whole range of names showed no understanding of risqué, sexual or scatological humour in English-speaking countries, or of the existence of simple language and cultural problems.

So the problem of working just in our own language is not only one of limited understanding; it's also one of limited and often disastrous communication. The effect is easy enough to see if we imagine making gaffes of a similar kind ourselves. In conversation you probably wouldn't know, because in many of the cultural traditions in Asia people wouldn't laugh to your face, nor would they tell you, but they might have a good laugh at your expense behind your back. For business or in govern-ment the effect might be more serious. Many times I have seen visiting delegations from Asian countries handed on arrival in Australia an itinerary in English. Imagine the boisterous obser-vations and laughing and falling about if a group of Australian politicians arriving in Beijing were handed their itinerary in Chinese.

The remedy is ultimately for Australians to learn Asian languages. But one might object that taking on a foreign lan-guage at a mature age and in the full stride of a professional career is too formidable an undertaking. Would it not be better to use interpreters and translators, thereby avoiding horrendous linguistic blunders? There are problems with this approach. How do you know if your interpreter or translator is any good? How do you know that what is conveyed is accurate and felicitous? The translations of Chinese toilet paper names were presumably quite acceptable to the Chinese management. Nothing can make you feel quite as uncomfortable in a foreign country as the feeling that something you have said or someone has said on your behalf, but do not understand, is making you look foolish.

Of course, it is possible to acquire knowledge by reading everything you can get your hands on about the country in English—about the society, the culture, the literature. We must do this too. I have long believed that seminars for business people, instead of being only on 'Doing Business with . . .' ought to focus on the intellectual and artistic currents and the social milieu. This would give business people, and politicians, a much better basis for understanding why the Chinese Government did what it did in Beijing in 1989, for example, or a framework for analysing what is happening now in Indonesia.

But in the end, there is no escaping the imperative of learning the language. Remember that the ancient concept of lingua franca refers to the language of a dominant power, usually in enforced occupation of other lands and in total inequality, and in its modern usage it has also been applied to dominant military, political and economic powers. What happens when there is another dominant power with a different language? What happens if we want relationships of equality? What should we do?

For the major languages of the region, there are now readily accessible programs in most Australian universities and in other institutions, both for award and non-award purposes. Many of these can be tailored to the individual requirement and take account of the need to provide flexible learning paths through combinations of intensive and regular teaching modes.

Total fluency takes time, but from 30 years of observing what goes on in Asian countries, I am certain that with intelligence, sensitivity and curiosity even a small amount of language brings inestimable benefits in communication and in access to the society. In most Asian societies people will commend and help your efforts to communicate in their language. Knowing the language also allows you to gauge the real performance and worth and loyalty of an employee, colleague, partner or friend.

The National Policy on Languages in 1987[20] was an encouraging development which helped education systems to begin to redress the lowly place to which languages had sunk in Australian schools. National direction, supported by federal funding, made a start in giving languages the place they should have in any civilised society. But in 1991 the government issued a White Paper on languages which dodged the issue of focus and priority in the selection of which languages to resource.[21] Australian leaders could not make up their minds because they were more concerned with sectional multicultural opinion than with the long-term future of Australia. In 1994 it seemed for a moment that we had recovered this situation, with the COAG decision in Hobart to commit all Australian jurisdictions to serious mainstreaming of Asian languages. But the federal bureaucrats and then the government temporised on funding of this program, and the Coalition Government is thinking of abandoning it altogether. This is to look not forward to 2020 but back twenty years.

But a goal of substantial language learning is achievable. Thirty years ago, 45 per cent of Australian school students were studying a foreign language. Of course, much of it was badly taught. So also was much of English, Science and Mathematics. Today the Australian figure is about 13 per cent; in Britain the number is about 50 per cent, and since 1992 the European Union has aimed to have all students studying two foreign languages.

The National Policy on Languages, of course, produced tensions. Some ethnic community representatives opposed 'the primacy of English as the national language and ethnic community languages as secondary' and the 'priority [given to] the languages of our trading partners, especially Asian languages'.[22]

There are two points to make about these tensions. One is that there should be no place in public policy or public debate for dichotomous or adversary positions between the various language interests. European versus Asian, cultural versus economic, or whatever other mutually antipathetic division, is no way to go for anyone seriously interested in reopening the Australian mind to language learning. Indonesian is no more an 'economic' language than Italian is 'cultural', and if we are concerned about what goes into the vocabulary of debate we must be concerned also to take these dogmas out. There must be common cause. The other point, however, is that Australia does have to make decisions about many things which involve choice and selection, in many matters, and education, and language in particular, can be no exception. It is similarly unhelpful to the language cause, therefore, and totally unrealistic, to suggest that all languages must be equally supported. It is hard enough supporting and resourcing just a handful of languages. Language offering cannot give parity of provision across the 47 or so languages which are to one extent or another in the education systems of this country.

The United Kingdom or France or Germany or Italy would not have any problem in arriving at decisions on which languages are important for them. They have made their decisions, as have other nations. People who speak Asian languages in Europe also speak other languages of Europe, and I hope that one day people who speak European languages here might also speak Asian languages. But there is a limit to the number of languages which can receive support from the public purse, even in economically strong countries. Choices have to be made. In Europe, no one suggests that all languages spoken in one country ought to be equally supported, a suggestion which has been voiced in Australia by some ethnic community leaders and some of the dogmatists of multiculturalism. The foreign languages students choose in Europe are, of course, from a small range of languages selected for their capacity to foster social and economic interaction *within* the European Union. We live in Asia. And that ought to be the determinant in our choice of languages.

Notwithstanding the many false starts, within the State and Territory education systems foreign language teaching is at least on the move. This is in part from social and parental pressure. In all States and Territories there are language policies and implementation plans, and some are putting funds towards implementation. Asian languages are high and often highest on the list of priorities, but other languages such as French, German, Spanish and some major community languages are also included. But it is even more important that we reopen foreign language learning to the mainstream, to large numbers of Australian students.

In the end, if we can put the humanities back into education, and regenerate the idea that an educated person is a literate one, and have sensible choices made about which languages ought to be fully supported by the public purse, and have these languages available commonly in schools and universities and well resourced and well taught, I don't really mind much which languages are taught, because many people will be learning the ones that matter nationally and some of these will be Asian and some will be European. But there must be some emphasis on Asian languages for nationally important reasons and to bring them up to the level of European languages. I suspect, however, that if we do not take the path I suggest, the tensions will persist, funding will be dissipated, and the language cause will not prosper.

The study of Asia, as distinct from the study of Asian languages, presents more difficult problems, and while the Hobart Declaration of the Australian Education Council[23] was categoric about languages, its statement that there should be 'an understanding and appreciation of Australia's historical and geographic context' is at best ambiguous.

Similarly, while education systems' documents and curriculum guidelines appear to offer the opportunity to study Asia, given the level of teacher expertise in Asia and the devolution of decision-making in curriculum to school or classroom level, students are learning little. But in the short to middle term at least, if Australians are to understand anything about Asia (let us say at least to understand articles in the better-quality newspapers and weeklies or informed comment on radio or TV), then it will be because they learn about it through the medium of English in the humanities and social sciences. Asian languages pose great demands of intellect and time on learners, and it would be foolish to believe that a few years of marginal high school Japanese or Chinese will equip students to come to terms with historical, political and economic concepts in the target language. I stress that 'studies' is not an easy substitute for Asian languages in terms of national needs. We do need, desperately, linguists and many people with a range of different language skills. But all Australians should be familiar with the history, geography, economics and politics of the region in which they live, and it is the study of Asia through these other disciplines which will provide that.

It is perhaps even more difficult to do something about 'studies' than it is about languages in an education system where there are no matters of belief or sense of the importance of national purpose and national direction. The difficulty lies in persuading people who are already in education to open their subject, their discipline and their minds to the existence of Asia. It is as important for scientists and mathematicians and doctors, or for that matter real estate agents or State Government public servants to be Asia-literate as it is for diplomats, or business people, or university carpetbaggers hawking education services around the region. Or people who may never encounter Asia in Asia.

And it is critical that 'studies' should develop within subjects and disciplines, as part of the history or the philosophy, across the spread of mainstream education, squarely in the central content. It is in my view wrong to set up 'Asian Studies' islands in physical mirror of the intellectual confinement to which we have condemned the many worlds of Asia.

It also ignores the lessons of power in education. I hear Asia in the words of politicians. I see Asia in the plans and programs of the Commonwealth Government and the universities and the State education sytems. But it is not yet in the power structures of the universities, for the most part, or in the education systems, or the schools, where the opening of the Australian mind to Asia has to begin. Because an essential element is still missing: there is no partnership between Australians for a shared vision for our education, for the real Australianisation of Australian education.

The issues of Asia, and the study of it, and immigration,

are the principal currents which will shape us over the next generation. I think we must turn John Hardy's proposition around. It is the region that will define us, not us it. I have no objection to that, if we are prepared and if we do not surrender on the non-negotiable. Our immigration is flowing strongly from the Asian region, and I have no objection to that either, provided all immigrants make a commitment to Australia, do not disparage Australian society, or say it has no culture, or see nothing to be valued, or bend it to ways which erode the nature of that which made it attractive to them as a place of settlement.

But if we are not intellectually prepared, we will not understand what is happening to us, we will not be participants in defining what it is to be an Australian or what visions are going to follow. We will be witting parties, through our own mental lassitude, to the surrender of equity in the intellectual determination of our future.

CHAPTER 6

The Asia-literate society

The idea of an Asia-literate society was first introduced by the Asian Studies Council in 1988. But the instrument by which this goal will have to be achieved is the Australian teaching force, which has not been prepared for Asia. Teachers are also undervalued and underpaid, and often demoralised. They also have had their fair share of bludgers, whingers and anti-intellectuals whose voices more often than not command the attention of ill-educated journalists, whose headlines in turn have contributed greatly to the lowering of esteem for what ought to be our most treasured and nurtured profession. This is the instrument which must deliver to us the Asia-literate society. But it is a resource which is struggling simultaneously on so many other fronts for its own reform and rehabilitation that its capacity to deliver what we need cannot be assured.

It is worth some attempt at a definition of 'Asia-literate'. In general I suggest this means:

1   that above all we should be armed with knowledge through rigorous, sustained and in-depth learning, and exposed to the ideas of Asian societies, and challenged by these ideas to examine our own;
2   that we should have acquired a cultural framework within which to relate to and understand Asian societies, to the

same extent as we have now with Britain and Europe, and which gives us the points of reference, the signposts, to address what is unfamiliar and to cope with it;

3 that we should know enough about the history and culture and geography and literature to be able to place Asian countries in context when we read about them in the press or meet their people or go there on a visit, and to be not completely lost in commonplace verbal and literary allusions;

4 that we should be able to function in an Asian society and communicate with Asian people without embarrassment or insecurity or condescension, and with understanding of their attitudes and prejudices and sensitivities;

5 that we should know enough to be informed participants in the Australian political process where that touches on Australia's interests in Asia;

6 that we should be able to enjoy our engagements with Asian societies and Asian people; to learn, to benefit, to enrich our own lives; share the same jokes; and

7 that our literacy in things Asian should be an asset in employment.

We need to be clear-headed in the use of the term. Some have replaced it or used it interchangeably with 'Asia-competent'. That is different. Mere competence will not give us what we need to come to terms with our Asian milieu. It will not even make us, in Asia, a clever country.

THE CENTRAL ROLE OF THE TEACHER

There has of course been a considerable shift in the definition of the professional role of the teacher in our society in the last few decades. In general, education has moved from a position where, dominated by a Christian ethos, young children were drilled in the basic skills of literacy and numeracy for external purposes, to one in which the centrality of a child is paramount, and education is 'facilitated' by a teacher who may devise an individual curriculum for each child, valid in terms of both the broad thrust of curriculum and the role and expectations of teachers. Some years ago, learning, both content and process, was highly defined, with outcomes monitored by a regulation-bound education bureaucracy exemplified by the inspector. Now we have a fluid situation in which learning 'guidelines' are interpreted by schools, teachers and children. Monitoring either by an inspectorate or external assessment until Year 12 is a thing of the past.

There is no doubt that the forbidding atmosphere which used to characterise much of education was undesirable. Challenge is desirable; fear is not. But with Dewey's pragmatism and the psychological movement in the 1920s and 30s and the swing towards child-centredness and learning as pleasure, Western education underwent a revolutionary change, which reached fruition in the United States, Britain and Australia in the 1970s and early 80s. This change produced something which Allan Bloom describes in *The Closing of the American Mind* as 'openness'.

Bloom speaks of openness in two ways. The first is teaching about what we (humankind) have achieved in a way in which all human activity and learning is deemed to be of equal value; Plato and photography, history and home economics are all on the same plane. This form of openness is reflected in the curricula and timetabling in our schools. It is true that mathematics, science and English have a core subject status in Australia. But the humanities and social sciences generally are left to the area of choice, where some or none may be studied to a meaningful level. In any case, content in these subjects is 'open'; that is, the process is the driving force and content merely serves the process. Bloom's second form of openness is a discriminating one. It makes judgments about what is valuable and even accepts the need for 'prejudices', in the sense of beliefs or value judgments, but then subjects these beliefs and judgments to a rigorous intellectual examination in the Socratic tradition: armed with knowledge and plagued by doubt. Such openness denies concepts like cultural relativism and forces stances on issues which are not easy to resolve but require a principled view which leads to one form of action rather than another.

In the context of Australia and Asia this latter is what we must do, and we must do it at two levels of consciousness. The first is to accept that Asia has a lot to teach us about what Western culture would call 'the good', the search for meaning and truth in a moral and ethical framework. To deny that is to deny the traditions of two-thirds of humankind, and to deny too the huge debt which the West owes to Eastern knowledge. The West's period of ascendancy has been quite brief and was fuelled to some extent by Eastern science and technology. In

Asian eyes, the last few hundred years are a pause, a depletion of energy, and Asia is now on the move again and taking in Western science and technology, evolving once more into cultures which are strong and resilient. For this reason alone, we must incorporate them into our learning. The second level is to accept the fact that we live in Asia, and if we are going to survive it will be by being knowledgeable about Asia, by being Asia-literate.

What, then, are the demands on education? I would suggest two necessary preconditions. The first is that there has to be a clear view of curriculum if we are to create an Asia-literate Australia; that is, we have to give Asia a non-negotiable place in the curriculum. The second is that until the curriculum for Asia-literacy is defined in some way there is little that can be done in the area of teacher education. Beyond the study of Asia, it is time to give serious thought to what the humanities and social science education of a young Australian ought to look like at the end of twelve years of schooling and what a teacher education program would look like to produce teachers who could deliver that. At the moment it appears to be rather *ad hoc*.

I am not concerned here only with the Asian content of the curriculum but with teacher commitment to teach about Asia. Teachers teach what they know and admire or perhaps love. Without that sense of commitment very little learning will take place. We have to ask *what it is that will cause teachers to want to teach about Asia and what it is that will cause children to want to learn about it.* While all education is a chancy business, my guess is that highly motivated, knowledgeable, highly Asia-literate teachers will attract students to their subjects. While there are both extrinsic and intrinsic factors in motivation, in the end it is the teacher who can convey a constant intimation of what is intrinsic, who carries students to explore that aspect of life. Of course we have to live in the real world and accept that most teachers will not operate at quite that level. But it is important to make the point that Asia-literacy is not a mere graft of another language or social science knowledge onto a would-be or serving teacher. Motivation is vital.

Extrinsic motivation does have its place. There should be adequate rewards for spending a great deal of time learning a language. Similarly, students or teachers who take on the study of Asian societies in various disciplines should feel that their labours are recognised. Language proficiency pay, scholarships, study leave, advanced skills status, academic qualifications can all provide motivation and should at least match the level provided for French and German. But more than that, for teachers of Asia the connection should be as close as it is for British teachers who teach the languages and cultures of Europe. There must be language training and upgrading within Australia, and frequent visits to Asia through institutional and other links. All of this will cost money, but the returns in quality teachers with commitment will be worth it. And in the long run we will reap the economic and other benefits which accrue from close ties with Asian countries. The Germans and French have known for a long time that education is an arm of diplomatic and commercial policy. We have to understand that too.

Motivation in education is critical, for both teachers and students. The fact is that ultimately all education is ultimately self-education, and extrinsic factors such as 'the national interest' or 'economic imperatives' are right for politicians and policy-makers, but, as suggested earlier, have little relevance in the classroom. That being said, I do believe that the teachers who teach our children should have, as professionals, a sense of the national interest, including the economic imperatives which will undoubtedly influence Australia's future.

This leads me to a proposition which is not always popular with education systems in Australia, which is that if the study of Asia is a national concern then the approach to it should be national. I do not mean by this that there should be central control through Commonwealth mechanisms but rather that, given limited resources, the systems must collaborate to decide what it is that constitutes the profile of Asia-literacy in terms of teacher education. Further collaboration with the tertiary system would refine that into teacher education programs which could be delivered across the nation, in a variety of modes, including distance education, for both pre- and in-service needs. By doing this we could harness the considerable intellectual forces in Australia to produce quality materials based on commonly agreed objectives and outcomes with national, portable accreditation. To go our separate ways is not nationally intelligent; if we are going to amount to anything in this region we are just going to have to act nationally. To do otherwise is to self-destruct.

Languages

In the area of languages, it is obvious that there are major problems associated with the level of language proficiency for teachers. In some States there is no proficiency requirement for teachers to become registered as language teachers. Thus teachers who are incompetent in all the macroskills—listening, speaking, reading and writing—are asked to teach a language 'communicatively'. To do this is to invite failure. Children are not fools. They very soon know if their teacher cannot read Chinese or Japanese or if they cannot conduct a simple conversation with a native speaker. Language proficiency is not like proficiency in other subjects, because in the learning situation it is both the means and the end. The teacher *must* be highly proficient. One of the reasons language learning in schools has declined has been because there have been inadequate or, more often, no criteria for the registration of a language teacher. Thus many language teachers, including teachers of such well-resourced languages as French and German, have not had the necessary proficiency to teach the subject in a school. For Asian languages the situation is even worse. It takes about three times longer to reach a given level of language proficiency in Chinese and Japanese than it does in European languages, so five years at school or a first year university course are a painfully inadequate preparation for a teacher of these Asian languages.

In what is currently achievable in a regular first degree in Australia, at the end of the third year graduates in Chinese and Japanese cannot read everyday literature such as newspapers, and certainly not novels or works of reference. They cannot write a business letter or even a long personal letter, they cannot understand the news on television or a conversation on everyday topics conducted between two native speakers, and they cannot speak the language with any fluency. What is lacking is something between a year and two years in a country where the language under study is spoken. But what is also needed is excellent teaching.

The implications for the education of language teachers are profound. In the first place, there is an overwhelming case for the introduction of a four-year first degree for Asian languages with a minimum of one year spent in a country where the target language is spoken. But of course the implications do not stop there. While it is true that general language proficiency is the goal, the teacher must have language to a level which will guarantee effective teaching and learning in the classroom. In other words the language learnt by a would-be teacher should to some extent be classed as language for a special purpose. Most Asian language courses in tertiary institutions do not give teachers that sort of competence. It follows that all tertiary language courses should have a proficiency rating, with proficiency testing of graduates as part of accreditation.

In terms of professional studies, there needs to be a rapid upgrading of the place Asian languages have in departments of education, with studies in linguistics, curriculum and method *specific to that language*. At the moment, the professional studies seem to be dominated by European languages, with a few hours of tutoring specific to that language, often delivered by a part-time tutor recruited from the school system. While this latter activity is no doubt useful, it does not constitute the basis for the award of a professional qualification. The Diploma of Education too needs some restructuring. The German model is appealing, with a two-year mixture of academic and supervised practical work.

Our registration of teachers should be seen against these criteria. Those who do not match the criteria should not be given registration, or, in special circumstances, should be given provisional registration while they complete their qualifications within a set time limit. Teachers who are not fully qualified should be paid much less than professional wages. Those who meet the minimum or are beyond that should be well rewarded.

We have to escape from the notion of the teacher as a generalist dogsbody with low-level skills. We still accept levels of competence in the classroom which would outrage us if they applied to our doctor, our accountant or even our plumber. The language teacher is the model for the student. The only model which is acceptable is that of the highly proficient specialist, because it is only at that level that the specific intrinsic motivation factors will come into play with students, based on respect and admiration and the desire to emulate their teachers.

In language teaching there should be no difference in expectations between primary and secondary teachers. The curious notion that professional skills, especially academic skills, should somehow be at a lower level for primary teachers is simply untenable. The implications for the teaching of primary school teachers are also profound and timely. The fragmented 'bitsa' courses which constitute the training of the Australian primary school teacher are in urgent need of reform. At the middle and upper level, particularly, teachers should have solid academic expertise. It follows that there should be more specialised teaching at this level.

Australia is of course already desperately short of Asian language teachers, particularly of Japanese, but, if we are to reach minimum targets, of Chinese and Indonesian too, and Korean and Thai and Vietnamese. This is one of the excuses given by politicians and officials in Canberra for backing away from commitment to the language effort. Some would fill the gap by using native speakers, either resident in Australia or recruited from overseas. I am in favour of the use of native speakers. They have a variety of roles, especially in immersion courses which cannot be replicated by teachers who are second-language learners. They provide not only authentic language but authentic socio-cultural opportunities which can only enrich students' learning. Having said that, there are some caveats which a combination of experience and research have indicated need to be taken into account.

In the first place, the teaching of one's first language as a second or foreign language is a highly skilled task, as is evident by the length of training given to teachers of ESL (English as a Second Language). Unless native speaker graduates are given equivalent training it is unlikely they will be successful in Australia.

Second, such native speakers have to deal with what is euphemistically called 'the Australian classroom situation'. This covers everything from the linguistics and methodology problems outlined above, to the capacity to handle 30 or more boisterous Australian adolescents who do not have a culture-inbred respect for teachers and who can destroy both learning and the teacher because they sense a 'lack of control'. If we ignore this we will produce even more problems. A related point is that there is a mutual loss of respect between teachers and students, and a loss of respect by the students for language learning.

Third, inappropriately qualified native speakers are often a kind of under-class in our teaching institutions, perceived as such by students and other teachers, and further contributing to the perception that languages are a kind of under-subject.

The last point is that we *must not* see the importation of foreign teachers as a cheap and expedient means of overcoming our deficiency. For the deficiency is not only a lack of teachers to carry out an urgently needed task. Imports are also a means of avoiding the task of training non-native Australian speakers in Asian languages. Australia has often looked overseas for trained workers rather than training its own, and we are paying the price for that now. We have also traditionally not learned other languages. We must escape from these two dangerous cultural traits and take charge of our own destiny. Our children have to see that *we* have taken the trouble to learn another language and think it important enough to pass on to them as teachers. What we value they will value.

Asian studies

While complex and urgent, the Asian languages situation is relatively straightforward when compared with the teaching of Asian studies and the training of teachers in that field. This brings me back to the humanities and social sciences in Australian schools, which have been so ill served by a variety of educational and social movements. The devaluing of core subjects like history and geography, together with the fragmenting of an identifiable body of knowledge, has especially complex ramifications when it comes to Asian studies. It is into such a cultural and educational milieu that Asian studies has to make its way and find a niche. If almost everything is an 'option' it is bound to be ignored. My point is that until there is a national view of the humanities and social sciences entitlement of Australian school students, Asia-literacy will be marginal or nonexistent for most of our children. If we can redefine the common learning of Australian children in the humanities and social sciences, and in it give the study of Asia a secure and well-considered place, then it will be easier to say what we require for the education of teachers. It is possible to envisage at least two levels here. A minimum requirement is that teachers, primary and secondary, would be trained to teach the Asian part of the school curriculum. The courses would be devised precisely towards that end. Accreditation and registration would depend on passing this. A corollary, of course, is that if intending teachers and teacher education institutions knew what the humanities/social science curriculum and job specifications were, then the courses could be more precisely tailored and nationally applicable.

The second level would be for people who were Asia specialists in particular disciplines and who had a strong commitment to Asia. These people would not only find places in the 'lighthouse schools' and 'centres of excellence' which seem to be an evolving idea in some States, but also take on roles as curriculum developers, advisers and so on. There are unfortunately very few people of this ilk in schools, and few likely to be so in the future, unless teaching becomes a more rewarding career, both financially and in terms of social status and career paths.

Most of our serving teachers have little or no knowledge of Asia, and they will constitute the bulk of our teaching force for the next twenty years. There is a problem of how to give them that strand to their professional qualifications. I think there must first be an atmosphere in which new learning for teachers is valued. It is not there in salary scales, where people with better qualifications are not rewarded, in either salary or enhanced prospects of any sort. So what we have is a largely static teaching force which in terms of being equipped to educate the children and workers of the next decade and the twenty-first century is deficient in training and in resources as far as Asia is concerned.

The training of language teachers is an example. To the extent that any department has done anything about Asian language teachers, this consists of using teachers of European languages, and methods which are derived from teaching those languages, in one or two cases with an Asian 'language adviser', and simply applying them to the unfortunates who are about to be thrust into the Australian classroom. We need them now to take a lead to develop the information base on the teaching of Asian languages as foreign languages.

THE ASIA-LITERATE SCHOOL

The Asia-literate teacher needs to be in the Asia-literate school. What should this school look like? What should it do?

There are two things which should not be done. The first is that in the Asia-literate school not every child will learn an Asian language all the way through school, and I think schools need to be careful about leading with an Asian language before they have really worked out what it is they want to be doing about Asia. The second is that the Asia-literate school would not have a subject called Asian Studies.

The reason why I caution against these approaches is that there must be a planned and intellectually and educationally

and socially defensible approach to Asia in the school. Each
school must understand why it is setting out to become an
Asia-literate school, and what that entails for every child in the
school. And the only defensible approach is one which offers
Asia to all students.

If we are to have an Australia-centric education, with Asia
in the curriculum for the reasons I have outlined, then all
children should meet Asia logically and naturally in the subjects they study, from primary school onwards, and across the
range of subjects, from Social Studies or Social Science and its
various parts, to the humanities, and Art and Music, and even
including Maths and Science. Asia does not have to be in every
subject every day. It does not have to be a subject on its own,
within a discipline, like 'Indonesian politics'. It just has to be
there, as part of the subject, so that students will imbibe it
naturally. And Europe does not have to move out. To suggest
that it must is either a dishonest opposition to the study of Asia
or a defensive argument of the feeble-minded. Europe does not
have to move out, but it does have to move over.

We must be very clear on one point: putting Asia into
education does not and must not mean putting into the classroom a dozen more 'cultures' alongside a dozen or so which
may be there already, and saying we value them all equally
but at the same time treating them as 'soft' learning. That
belongs to the ideological end of multiculturalism, and is one
of the most unintellectual currents Australia has seen. What I
am talking about is rounded intellectual development, through
the infusion of Asian content into mainstream subjects. Not
dogmatically, not separately, but differentiating one Asian culture from another and evaluating and judging its worth and
contribution, and encouraging children to understand that in
the human experience there is no such division as a subject
called History which includes British and European and American and Australian history and then some separate and unrelated thing called Indonesian history or Asian history, that there
is no global subject of politics which does not include the
politics of Asian states, that art and philosophy and religion are
universal matters in which the contribution of non-European
cultures may sometimes be greater than that of Europe, and
sometimes the other way round.

I am familiar with the arguments against infusion in this
and many areas of learning. But to set up a subject called Asian
Studies is to invite children to believe that everything to do

with Asia is somehow different from mainstream human experience. The Australian experience has shown that it is invariably seen as peripheral, and marginal. It ought therefore to be educationally unacceptable. And it creates another problem: as a separate subject, it has to compete for time and preference and is unlikely to make headway in the jostling of subjects in today's schools. Experience across many schools over the last twenty or so years has shown that the very existence of a subject called Asian Studies ensures that the matter of Asia will not be taken up in mainstream subjects. A subject called Asian Studies therefore usually defeats the purpose of the Asia-literate school.

Nor should the teaching about Asia given in such a school be primarily about things like 'village life in Java', although that is an obvious component of what might be taught about Indonesia. The 'village life in . . .' kind of subject matter, if it is isolated from the urban and the contemporary and the high culture and great achievements of the society concerned, and the things we can relate to as being in common, tends to present Asia as totally removed from the real world of our own experience and thereby to put it back into that category of quaint, marginal, backward and inferior, a presentation not all that far removed from the nineteenth-century paternalism from which our Britannia-centric education derives.

What then should be embodied in the Asia-literate school? It would, in the first place, be Australia-centric and committed to hard culture (see Chapter 5).

Second, it would have a shared idea of what is meant by being Asia-literate. The school will want to define what this means in more specific terms, but it also needs to be clearheaded in the use of the term.

Third, the school would offer at least one Asian language, in a structured sequence through every year of the school, whether it is primary or secondary. Up to the fourth year of high school, most should study a language, and beyond that about 25 per cent.[24] The language teaching and assessment would distinguish between first- and second-language learners. It would also distinguish between and address many levels of proficiency for different purposes, and recognise that some students will not achieve fluency or command but can still acquire a working knowledge of the language and benefit from that acquisition. Proficiency scales *must* be user-driven. Unless they tell the student and the potential employer precisely what they can do with the language they have learnt, they are useless.

The choice of language is important. It should ideally come from an assessment of the overall objectives and strengths of the school in teaching about Asia. If History and Geography and Art and other subjects are strong enough to support, for example, Thai, or if the school has a clear policy to develop that strength, then it could choose Thai. But it should not decide that Thai is 'in', and then spend the next few years trying to work out how to support it with teaching in other subjects by teachers who have no knowledge of, or even interest in, Thailand.

I think we should also have some reservations about introducing a language in a school just because of student demand. The demand for Japanese is great, but it cannot always be adequately resourced and is therefore not well taught. Similarly, just because a school catchment area contains many speakers of one language is not in itself reason for introducing a foreign language as essential to the curriculum. If current projections are valid, by the turn of the century Australia can hope to have only 25 per cent of secondary students learning an Asian language. And that will require a Herculean effort, and even if it is achieved, few will have mastery, a few more will have fluency, some numbers will know the language reasonably, but most will not achieve a very high standard. There will be those among them, I hope not too few, who will also be Asia-literate.

Fourth, for the rest of the student population, Asia-literacy will for the time being come mainly through other-than-language study. This feature of the Asia-literate school is one in which the study of Asia is available to all students, built in to the curriculum from primary school, and not just for those who opt for 'Asian Studies'.

Fifth, the school would have considerable interaction with Asia, drawing on people of Asian origin within the community and linking with Asia through institutional arrangements involving an active program of two-way exchanges. I know that links with Japan are burgeoning and understand why. But Japan is not Asia. Indonesia lies on our doorstep, and if the school's idea of that country is still poverty, peasants and padi, it will suffer a severe jolt when it finds that aspects of Indonesia are sophisticated, technologically advanced and economically developing at a rapid rate. The Philippines is just as close to Australia, and is a very accessible society, the only one, incidentally, between here and Japan with a truly free press. Korea, perhaps a bit like Australia, has been washed by competing cultures, and many Australians I speak to say they find much in common with Koreans, more so they would claim, than with Japanese or Chinese. Vietnam will offer extraordinary excitement to the student who is lucky enough to have his or her school take it up. And there are others, each with something important and distinctive to offer.

A sixth important requirement of the Asia-literate school is that Asia teachers must have a place in the decision-making structures of the school. When you look at what goes on in universities, and the failure of the study of Asia to make much headway beyond the islands of Asian Studies, you are struck by the fact that with perhaps two exceptions the Asia academics have virtually no power, no place in the power structures of the university. The same is true of most schools. This does not mean you have to stack the decision-making structures of the school. But so long as Asia teachers have no position or power, it is almost beyond doubt that the Britannia-centric model will continue to replicate itself.

THE ASIA-LITERATE TEACHER

How do we produce the Asia-literate teacher? The time has come for the faculties and departments of education in our universities to deliver. I know there are exceptions, and I know there are moves in some universities to address this problem. But if our universities in general are universities of British studies, the quintessence of this is to be found in Australian faculties of education. For the most part they have ignored Asia.

The training of language teachers is an example. But the problem does not end with language. Take primary school teachers, most of whom are still expected to be generalists and most of whom have only had a broad general education, in the British mould. What they add to their knowledge in their teacher training is critical. We need some course content which will enable them in their professional careers to lead primary students in their first steps towards Asia-literacy. Take secondary teacher training. We need from the teacher trainers a new kind of teacher qualified to teach about Asia. We need universities to research the matter, to identify problems, produce solutions, work out combined degrees with other faculties, make appointments of people with other than the conventional British or European background and qualifications. I have been involved in Asia in our education for 25 years, and never has it been so apparent that the problem keeps coming back to the universities in general and the faculties and departments of education in particular. This is something we must all take up in a helpful and constructive way. It cannot be left to the universities. Or to the State governments. Or to Canberra.

An important point here is that teachers will teach what is *required*, otherwise they will teach according to their personal inclinations, which is not what curriculum is about. The study of Asia needs to be infused into the humanities and social sciences through to Year 12—the washback effect from Year 12 on curriculum is tremendous. If Asia is seen to be a non-negotiable element of students' work at that level, then teachers will begin to incorporate its study much earlier. But I believe that there should also be a principled structure of Asian content built from primary through to secondary school rather than just using Year 12 content as a stick to cause change further down.

Even given the availability of structured curriculum and resources, there is still the problem of the retraining of the current teacher force. The ongoing professional development of teachers, and its relationship to accreditation and reaccreditation, is a question which needs to be urgently addressed. Some teachers constantly upgrade their qualifications, often with little or no support. Others have not studied in either their discipline or the professional field since they graduated ten, twenty or thirty years ago. In this *laissez faire* situation how do we cause and manage change?

The answer seems to lie in planned professional development for *all* teachers and a link with reaccreditation. This should also be linked with salary and with the award of postgraduate qualifications. In such a situation it is possible to see a national need, such as teaching about Asia, being able to be planned and implemented. This will require cooperation and collaboration between education systems, registration boards and tertiary systems across the nation. But I believe it can be done.

As to what a professional development package on the teaching about Asia content would look like, it should be:

- national, i.e. agreed by all parties involved;

- accredited by one or more tertiary institutions in each State or Territory;
- available in face-to-face and distance modes;
- equivalent to a semester-length postgraduate unit;
- related to accreditation/reaccreditation; and
- related to salary/promotion.

Asia teachers are used to being on the margin of school life. It is rare to have a community of Asia teachers in a school, unlike mathematicians, for example, or teachers of English or History. In the Asia-literate school, the community of Asia teachers would be different, because they would not be Asia subject teachers. Rather, most teachers in the school would have some familiarity with, and sometimes teach about, Asia, in the same way that they do now about Britain or Europe. They will need advisers, curriculum support and ongoing professional development within their systems. Information dissemination too will be a vital factor. It may be that here too systems could cooperate. It is essential that teachers feel supported in this work given the current level of development.

The goal of an Asia-literate society should be to nurture people who are well educated and wise enough to take on the most delicate and sensitive issues in Asia, as in Europe, in direct conversation and preferably in several languages, who have a capacity to understand why a very different view may be held is held in that society and why it is held strongly, who feel challenged by opposing ideas but who can argue firmly and without compromising principles which are important within Australia, and yet who can emerge with a personal relationship consolidated and enhanced. That is a challenge of a kind we don't often discuss. But that is the challenge which faces Australia, and the challenge which faces those who have the freedom and the responsibility to decide how to define and serve the goals of educating our children.

CHAPTER 7

A failure of leadership?

When I first went to work in Canberra, about 30 years ago, official contact with Asia was overwhelmingly through the departments of External Affairs, Trade, and the Prime Minister's Department, with the odd encounter from departments like Civil Aviation, Attorney-General's and one or two others, and the particularly odd encounters of Defence. State governments were still more interested in who got the position of agent-general in London, with the opportunity that gave, at public expense, to see the old country, get on the piss and talk to the Queen. A republican Australia? Think what that would do to these important diplomatic goals!

Today, every government department in Canberra and almost every Commonwealth instrumentality, every State government and every university has some kind of contact in the Asian region, as well as many of the people who administer local government, schools, and even government-supported community organisations. But the more the number of government departments involved in external relations has increased, the more the resources have been stretched beyond the few who are equipped with knowledge and understanding. Officials may have succeeded in persuading business to have a go at 'Asia', but they were unable to assist them to a refined understanding of different Asian markets, and there are not a few cases of squandering of public funds on uninformed and even farcical leading of business into quite unprospective fields in Asia. Even some basic knowledge of the geography of Asia could have helped to avoid some of these misguided endeavours. But the economic challenge in Asia was not to avoid mistakes. It was to enhance the Australian performance, and to do that it is necessary to know which market you are in and what makes one different from another. Studying Asian societies at school will not, of course, make a good business performer. But it will help to make a good one effective in an Asian commercial environment.

It comes back to the culture of the people who are involved in Asia, and in this the public administrator is crucially important. We are a long way from any kind of conceptualisation of what it should mean for this person—to be a public administrator in a Western country whose future will be determined in and by Asia. This is dangerously unmindful of the national interest. The nation needs attention to this question and a proper thinking out of the culture of our public sector institutions.

ASIA IN THE CULTURE OF THE PUBLIC SERVICE

The Department of External Affairs, subsequently Foreign Affairs, now Foreign Affairs and Trade, began in the early 1960s to recruit and to train people with specialist skills in Asian countries. That was good. But what it did not do negated the virtue of what it did. For more than two decades, it did not count these skills a virtue in the evaluation of a career officer's potential for mainstream senior or leadership appointment. On the contrary, it drew a distinction between the so-called generalist and the so-called specialist, and often explicitly held the two to be in some way mutually exclusive. To be highly literate and skilled in respect of an Asian country was somehow counted narrow (whereas the experience of achieving this, of getting there and being there, can be immensely broadening), while at the same time people literate and skilled in respect of, for example, France, were thought to be broad, and both specialist and generalist. For years there was no career path which said, 'if you have or acquire this special Asia literacy and skill, then here, other skills being present, is how you can see a career path which uses these attributes and can take you to the top'.

There is to this day no requirement that officers in this department *must* have a foreign language, still less an Asian language. I accept that language is not everything. But in *this* profession, and assuming intellect and skills in other matters, language is what *gets* you to everything. It is often also the brand of someone who has gone through a difficult test.

It is especially important in official dealings with other countries, because it allows effective two-way communication. The essence of the challenge of diplomacy is to be able to persuade someone else to your point of view or get them to do what you want them to do. But this requires that you understand the imperatives of their 'culture'. Within Australia, if you do not understand, for example, the culture of the ABC, or Treasury, or the University of Queensland, you will have the greatest difficulty in getting them to do what you want them to do. In one definition, 'a society's culture consists of whatever it is one has to know or believe, in order to operate in a manner acceptable to its members, and do so in any role that they accept for any one of themselves'.[25] The challenge of another 'culture' is really the hard part of diplomacy. The department's way of handling culture as such has been as bilateral arts exchange, and not in developing a departmental culture which ensures that its officers are well enough acquainted with Asia to operate in a manner acceptable to the members of Asian societies, 'in any role that they accept for any one of themselves'. By this I do not mean that our diplomats are diplomatic oafs, or insensitive or unintelligent, or do not work hard at trying to learn about and understand Asian countries. Many do work hard at this and also take on Asian languages. It is the departmental culture and what it does or does not demand of its diplomats that is of concern here. It was not until 1994, for example, that the department first introduced cross-cultural communication training (in English) for its officers.

The second thing External Affairs did not do was to push other departments in Canberra into recruiting, giving value to and promoting Asia-literate and Asia-skilled people. There were those in the department who had been out there in the front line and knew it mattered. But I suppose that if its own culture was not itself so fashioned, it was impossible that the department could have promoted such change in the corporate culture of others.

The third thing the department did not do was to become an agent for change in mainstream, grassroots education. Any democratic country's foreign policy requires a supporting constituency, and where change is involved the constituency must be knowledgeable, and informed. The burning of the Indonesian flag in Australian demonstrations over Timor in late 1995 provides an illustration. It may be legal to burn someone else's flag, but the Australian electorate has not been educated to understand the complex balancing off of issues and interests that goes on in the relationship with Indonesia. Burn if you like (I don't find it acceptable or necessary), but at least understand what you might be endangering or sacrificing at the same time. This episode dramatically illustrated the great gap between policy and the political constituency in relation to Asia. I raised it as an issue of national concern with Government and Opposition, but while there was concurrence there has been no subsequent initiative to bring the public into greater awareness of the balance of interests in foreign policy issues.

It would have been greatly to the national good if we had started 30 years ago to change the content of education and thereby to create a broadly informed constituency. Education is not, of course, the brief of Foreign Affairs, but even the initiative which created the Asian Studies Council in the mid–1980s came from the then Department of Trade, also not responsible for education.

The Commonwealth Department of Education,[26] which does have the responsibility, bears a much greater burden of culpability than any other administrative body in Australia. The Asian Studies Council showed that you can induce fundamental change in education at the grassroots from the centre, even when they tell you school education is a State responsibility. Under its various names over the past 30 years this part of our federal public administration did almost nothing, until very recently, to produce an education to fit Australia for a future with Asia.

When the Asian Studies Council was created in 1986 there were possibly only two people, apart from the minister, who even wanted it. Those responsible for it moved to control and limit the council's role and then recommended, and secured, its extinction. The secretariat which replaced it was then disbanded. This may not be surprising because there is no requirement for Asia-literate or language-speaking officers and certainly no career path for such people in this department. I had the greatest difficulty explaining to those in Asia with whom this council had built relations and programs, some with their money, why Australian officials had whimsically decided to eliminate the body Australia had set up to change the education to change the cultural norms to fit the populace to become part of Asia. After five years. It was but one of the many confusing signals we sent to Asia over this period.

We may think some Asians inscrutable. We are at times nationally inexplicable.

The administrators in our universities in general have also taken Asia quite casually; those from whom we expect leadership have been followers. And the administrators in universities only discovered Asia when the export of education brought business-class travel, five-star Asian hotels, shopping in Hong Kong and the joys or woes of Patpong Road in Bangkok. This resulted in the late 1980s in one of the most demeaning episodes in the history of Australia in Asia: university administrators elbowing each other out of the way off the QANTAS plane to get the best stand in some tawdry display of the supposed best of Australia's education wares, offering without discrimination, to the highly discriminating Asian potential student, everything from the most outstanding and world-beating our universities had to offer to the detritus on the seabed of the intellectually and academically remaindered.

State governments also must not escape responsibility for what has not happened in education. It is they, after all, who administer the public school systems. And their contribution until the last few years has been unsystematic, spasmodic and largely at the optional margins of education. With two singular exceptions, the Northern Territory and Queensland, there was no broad philosophical, conceptual, intellectual or pedagogical framework within which State school systems could develop the study of Asia as part of the entitlement of all schoolchildren.

A second major problem for which public administrators bear significant responsibility is the relative absence of public discussion about Asia and the slow decline in the quality of media contribution to that discussion. It used to be said that foreign policy issues were peripheral to Australian politics except at election times, when Reds under the bed was about as high as the 'debate' ever got. We may have been able to get away with that when Australia still felt it could work within the cocoon of an alliance, and just get on with trading with white friends on the other side of oceans and continents.

In the uncertain world of today that will not do. Our close relationships are greater in number and diversity. They are also more sensitive, and bring problems like the one we have had with Malaysia. Not to have done something about the level of debate is to have been irresponsible about our future in Asia and therefore about our future itself. Australians, of course, are not good at this sort of thing. In immigration, for example, when the debate has got under way it has been killed because it doesn't suit someone's political agenda. We seem to have had no sense of sustained public debate being a good thing, even if it does go against our views.

The Australian public has needed to understand the full implications of what is meant by an engagement with Asia. It has therefore needed to be infinitely better informed about Asian countries and regional issues. And while this placed a great demand for information and intellectual input on the media, there is much that the public administrator could have done to nurture discussion. It is not surprising, therefore, that when debate does flare, on Asian immigration, or human rights in China, or the State Law and Order Restoration Council (SLORC) in Myanmar or the assault on the opposition in Jakarta, it is ill informed to the point of being ignorant, and emotional rather than intellectual. And because government is not ready with intelligent information and intelligent networks into which this can be fed (as distinct from its political reactions), it is not surprising that the only way to handle the debate is to kill it.

I have a shiver of concern for the health of democracy in Australia when I hear ministers say that people should cease their criticism and get on with the job, concentrate on the big issues. This alerts us to the way in which we stifle debate. How often have public servants who frequent ministers' offices heard 'let's get it off the front pages'. The role of the public administrator ought to be to champion informed, reasoned and open debate, not to get it off the front pages.

There are several ways in which the fact of Asia can be absorbed into the culture of public administration. The first, and the earliest to appear in Australian institutions, is what might be called 'taking it on the run'. At its most superficial, this consists of the person who has been on a professional trip to Asia. Having been once, they may go again. And again. They turn up at interdepartmental committees, they are sometimes turned to for opinions on Asia, they are turned out to meet the delegations from China whose frequency has become an occupational hazard in Australian public life. They become the

organisation's Asia hand or—that dehumanising word—
'resource'. At its more substantial, the person who is the department's Asia 'resource' has had a posting in an Asian country.

This kind of on-the-job exposure was once the only means
by which the few institutions which had connection with Asia—
External Affairs, Trade and the Trade Commissioner Service,
the predecessors to AUSAID, and a small handful of other
Commonwealth and State agencies—acquired professional
'expertise' in Asia. It involved no training or schooling, no
language, no professional development. But it did provide some
accumulation of surface knowledge, a kind of human filing
cabinet in which you sometimes rummaged for miscellaneous
information.

There were in fact some people who through native intellectual capacity and application became quite outstanding Asia
hands by such means. They were one-offs, and this is no longer
an acceptable way to go about Asia, in terms of contemporary
thinking on professionalisation and having people properly qualified to meet the challenges of their job. But the fact is that
this remains, overwhelmingly, the principal means by which
Australian institutions have taken on the existence of Asia. And
it has almost no effect whatever on the thinking or the culture
of the institutions themselves.

The next stage has been the rise—but not the ascendancy—
of the person professionally qualified in something to do with
Asia, perhaps in the history or politics or economy of an Asian
country, perhaps speaking the language. This kind of person
started to appear in Australia about 30 years ago, and first
started turning up in the Department of External Affairs at
about the same time. Mostly they arrived in our institutions
already having these qualifications from the new Asia courses
then being established in our universities, but in the case of
External Affairs, the department also began to send selected
new recruits on courses in Australian universities, at the RAAF
Languages School at Point Cook, and sometimes overseas. I was
one of the beneficiaries of this program.

Now, although appropriate to the government's view of our
relations with Asia at the time, this practice also had virtually
no effect on the overall institutional culture, in External Affairs,
or in Trade. It added to the available knowledge, put some
quality into the filing cabinet, but these people mostly remained
just that, a kind of reference library which you sometimes
remembered you had and referred to, but never used to the full,

and never brought into play to help drive the thinking of the day's work as it related to Asia. This remained the case, in those few institutions which had primary carriage of our dealings with Asia, well into the 1980s.

The third stage, which emerged in a spotty way in the early 1980s and by the early 1990s was more or less fully operational in Foreign Affairs and Trade and in Austrade, less so in AIDAB, and only to a very limited extent in other agencies of Commonwealth and State governments, was the 'internalisation' of the skills of these Asia people, by now available in the increasing numbers of qualified graduates turning up in the recruitment process. Internally, these institutions began to understand that such people had value for the institution, could enhance performance and the attainment of the outcomes sought by the governments and management, and should be deployed in positions where they could best contribute to those outcomes. The appointment of Dr Ashton Calvert in December 1993 as ambassador to Tokyo—the first Japan-specialist, Japanese-speaking professional we have had in that post—was a high point in this development, and something of a watershed.

This internalisation represented the first real shift in the culture, at least of those agencies. What comes next?

The first point is the obvious but necessary one that, as already indicated, the Australian engagement with Asia has moved far beyond those few agencies of government which relate to what might once have been our 'external' portfolios. I know of no agency of government, Commonwealth or State, which does not now have connections of some kind with Asia. This is the natural outgrowth of our enmeshment with Asia in everything from meat to meteorology, and it will enlarge and intensify over the next generation. But take also the example of university administrations. Just about everything they do these days has an Asia dimension, from student recruitment and fund-raising to the administration of policies on exchange arrangements and research and teaching and placement, to the organisation of graduation ceremonies in Asian countries.

What is required now in our public sector institutions is that process of extending the intellect, broadening the culture, enriching the emotions and freeing up psychological conditioning that is implied in the term 'Asianisation' as I have used it earlier. The overall culture of public sector institutions has to be changed. Everyone needs to be educated in and acculturated to and skilled in matters to do with Asia, and not just the few;

the practice of taking it on the run, which is still the norm for most institutions, is not acceptable. The school of thought which says I can work anywhere across the Asian region solely with my European or Britannic culture and skills and using only English is, in the face of the professional tasks and challenges and importance to us of Asia, simply unprofessional.

It is fairly common now for Australian business to be told to get serious about Asia and give itself the skills to do so, and at least some of that emanates from public sector institutions. But these institutions themselves are just as much involved in the engagement with Asia, and in some cases the engagement is wider and deeper and the burden of responsibility more heavy. And some in business may be out in front of them. There are at least some corporate executives who say they have to change the overall culture of their corporations, the whole culture and not just that of the few who deal with Asia, and who recognise that this means serious programs of in-service training and education, and changes in the criteria for main-stream recruitment and promotion. There are already some who accept that this must include, and even begin with, all senior executives and management, and also, if that were possible, with the members of the board. This recognition is in itself a fantastic shift in thinking, and some corporations are already moving down the track in implementation.

I am not suggesting that every public official should have an Asian language now. Many should, and more will if the programs foreshadowed for schools begin to work their way through. Asian language skills do need to become common, however, to an extent that we must be able to conduct frontline engagements with Asia in an Asian language, and that we must always have enough people to hand to enable routine encounters to move into someone else's language rather than always being in our own. But for the medium term, for most public officials what is needed is the rigorous study of history or sociology or anthropology or politics or economics or ideas or literature or science, or many other things that go into 'hard' learning. I am not talking primarily here about the Department of Foreign Affairs and Trade. If I were, I'd be suggesting something much more intensive, because they are the professional service for dealing with the outside world and there is normally a different and more exacting set of professional criteria for a professional service. I am talking about officials in all public departments, from the arts, to education and research, to health care, the law, law enforcement, local government, the environment, industrial relations, or just about any other field of government activity, because relations with the Asian region are part of the portfolio responsibility of every department.

I am also not talking about creating armies of specialists. I am talking about creating armies of educated people among whom it is not regarded as specialist to be Asia-educated. The culture of public sector officials in respect of Asia should be similar to what it is in respect of the West or Europe: not specialist in any aspect of it, but deeply educated in it, literate, skilled, able to recognise and understand the signposts, qualified to take on the job. For those of us who grow up here—and we must remember and include the many who have not—there will always be more weight of background knowledge and culture and experience on the Western side than on the Asian. But the aim should be that it becomes as unacceptable in any of our public sector institutions to be uneducated in the culture of Asia as it would be today to be uneducated in the culture of the West.

If Australians are to be excellent in their dealings with Asia, education has to help prepare them to be so, not simply by making them informed and knowledgeable, but by helping to make them more international in outlook, more sophisticated, better able to take advantage of the opportunities they will meet in everyday situations. This is absolutely crucial in the education of officials at every level of government.

And we have to include the politicians. If the board of a business corporation needs this, so do ministers in governments, and all elected politicians. Australians are cynical about their politicians, and one of the great reasons for being cynical over the past decade or so is their urging on the populace skills upgrading and lifelong skilling while doing nothing about this for themselves. The Asia–Australia Institute has offered many times to both Labor and the Coalition in the Federal Parliament intensive briefings or short courses which would start the process of skilling. The response has always been positive, but nothing ensues.

If we think about this, the implications are very serious. If these people came to the Parliament skilled and literate in some aspect of Asia or some Asian language, which they do not, the unwillingness to engage in further skilling might be understandable but not excusable. But the failure of politicians to develop these nationally important skills, and to give leadership

by example, cannot continue without the most serious consequences for our capacity to handle our relations with Asia now,
and into the future. In China, which is generally thought to be
one of the most self-centred societies on the planet, numbers of
ministers and other leaders now speak a foreign language. The
same is true of Japan. In Indonesia there are ministers who are
fluent in several languages.

I believe there is no justification in 1996 for sending to a
major negotiation in one's own region a government minister
who is not fully literate in that region and fluent in the relevant
language. In Europe it would be at least unusual, possibly rare.
Similarly, it is frightening to think that a Cabinet which delib-
erates important domestic matters affecting our relations with
Asia, or is asked to consider policies which will have conse-
quential influence on our future with Asia, has next to no Asia
skill or literacy within its own ranks.

The Coalition Government has come to power after thirteen
years, and the world is much changed and the need to understand Asia much greater than when it was last in office. Not
least is the fact that the Asianisation of Asia has produced the
Asia which says no, including to Australia. If we fail to do
something about the education of these federal politicians, the
possibility that we will make right decisions about the matters
in the last chapter of this book is not great.

PROFESSIONAL EDUCATION IN ASIA

If Asianisation in the senses I have described earlier will equip
Australia to be a properly self-interested and street-wise, but
also sensitive and contributing, player in Asia, there is another
front on which we need to move, which is necessary to our
integration with the Asian region and for the fullest possible
participation in the development of the form Asia will take.
This is professional development undertaken in the Asian
region—that is, outside Australia, in an institution located in
East Asia and having a region-wide character and constituency—and the development of regional institutions which will
provide that. This also is a form of Asianisation, and as with
Asianisation within our own institutions, it will not be a threat
to our society or our identity but an enrichment. It does not
have to wait for the realisation of what I have described as
domestically necessary. But it cannot and must not be under-

taken by Australia alone or by solo Australian initiative. It may be, initially, more difficult, but I suggest that now is a good time to start on it.

And there is additional reason for this, which is external to Australia. Part of the discussion about Asia which is going on in other countries of the Asian region concerns the matter of where it is best to send people for professional training, as executives and managers, public and private. There is some questioning of the preference for training in North America and Britain and Europe, and of whether every good student needs to be sent out of the region for such training, and of whether what is offered there is in all respects appropriate for Asia. Part of the answer to this questioning will be found in the growth and strengthening of domestic institutions within these Asian countries, Australia included. But there is also a widely asked question: why do we not have more professional training institutions for the Asian region, and why do we not accord those which do exist greater prestige?

There is already the Asian Institute of Management in Manila and the Asian Institute of Technology in Bangkok, and there are numbers of national training institutions, including those in Australia, which recruit students throughout the region. But there are ideas circulating for the establishment of new regional professional training institutions which are not so nation-bound. My reading of this situation is that the demand will strengthen to a point where a number of new regional institutions of this kind will emerge over the next few years, and I believe the next step for Australia, in its regionalisation and Asianisation, is to move strongly into this current and undertake the professional training of many of its public sector people in such institutions. The benefits ought to be as obvious for the Asian context as are the benefits of an MBA or MPA undertaken in the United States for the United States context. But in Asia they will be more immediate for us, and more relevant to the direction of our economic and other policy interests.

I think we can also be a part of the formation of such institutions, but there are some cautionary notes. I hope this will not be seen as yet another opportunity for the export of Australian education. It is still the tendency of most education and training institutions in Australia to approach Asia by forays into the region, and to approach regional education as something in which you design a course for the region, whether for delivery at home in Australia or in Asia. There will always be room for this. But the problem is that behind that kind of initiative there is still often the thinking that Australians can do it better than Asians. We are of course very good at education, but there ought to be enough evidence by now to convince us that there are things that Asian societies do better than us or outstandingly well, and we should not make the assumption that whatever we have to offer in education is always better. What I am talking about has to be done in company with and with support from many Asian countries. For our own benefit it has to be done somewhere in the region and not in Australia, and it has to be done on the basis of equality of professional input among the partners.

Whether these new regional institutions have Australian partners or not, professional development and education in such schools is the ultimate stage for Australian institutions in making that passage from Europe to Asia, and very large numbers of Australian public administrators ought to be given the opportunity to experience it. If the process I have described for our institutions at home will domesticate us to the Asian habitat, this regional process will not only provide appropriate professional training for people who are to be involved as participants in a new Asia, it will bond them to the networks of power and influence which they will need to be effective in their professional careers.

This is why at the Asia–Australia Institute from the very beginning we have aimed at doing the bulk of what we do in the region. We have spent the best part of five years building the region-wide networks to support and guide us in this purpose. We have an active Council with councillors at very high levels of influence in every country of East Asia, and an East Asia forum comprising about 500 leading thinkers from the region, and an operational network which draws together a circle of like-minded institutes in each one of the countries of East Asia. In the course of establishing these connections we have found a high level of interest in new regional professional institutions, and this has encouraged us to begin discussions for a permanent school for professional education and training of executives from around the region. It has attracted widespread interest and support.

Australians are of course not alone in the process of Asianisation, and I would suggest that taking up this issue of Asianisation is not just another thing to be attended to in a crowded agenda for public administration, but one of the most exciting, and professionally rewarding, and for Australia most significant of all the things on that agenda.

CHAPTER 8

Values, ethics, business

I was asked by the St James Ethics Centre to give the centre's annual lecture, and the subject suggested was 'Ethical Dimensions of Australia's Engagement with Asian Countries'. This has resulted in a fruitful collaboration between the centre and the Asia–Australia Institute, including on a regional forum for the discussion of ethical issues. But the lecture topic gave me some problems. Much of what the St James Ethics Centre does has to do with helping business. Not exclusively by any means, but the focus is ethical problems, and the audience for the lecture was to be mainly business, and the professions which support or feed on them. I supposed that the audience would be expecting something on the problems faced by Australian companies in Asia, including the vexed issue of corruption, but this led me to thinking about several other matters.

One was that the ethical issue is not just a business issue but a national one, and how Australia (not the St James Centre, but Australia) has allowed business and economics to have such a dominant and leading position in our relations with Asia that it has actually pushed aside and obscured more important and fundamental human and philosophical things. For a truly humane and liberal society, this ought not to be acceptable. Business needs to be encompassed within the society and not the society within business. But in a way, the latter condition

124

is where we are and where we are headed, and it carries great dangers for the society. Another was whether many Australians have ever thought enough about what they believe in to know where they ought to draw the line if they had to in ethical and related matters in engagement with Asia. I am not suggesting that Australians or all Australian business people are 'unethical', although this is what the chief executive officer of one of our largest corporations inferred when I raised this question over a lunch, his inference confirming that he at least had not thought about it and did not even know what I meant. Another question was whether those who have thought about it and do know are in a position to do much about it in the national interest. And this led me in turn to try to see a conceptual framework for thinking about *this* issue in relation to the future, and Australia and Asia and the future, and these are the matters of the remainder of this book.

This chapter is about what I think about business and its role in our relationship with Asia, and the problems which stem from economism, the dogma that economics provides all the answers and must take precedence in all public policy. But it is really about values, and about reasserting the leadership of politics and culture and society, and human and philosophical concerns, over economics and business, in order to put values and ethics into a central position in what comes next in our history.

For most Westerners involved in engagement with Asian countries there are no ethical dimensions. This was so in the past. It may be even more so today, because the relentless advance in Asia of 'international' culture brings a kind of Western standardisation or homogenisation, of news and information, education, entertainment, taste, and even language. The banners of international culture, CNN for example, or McDonald's, are confirming. They comfort Westerners by suggesting that there is no difference for us to have to deal with, that the values are ultimately the same. Not yet all the same, of course, because we contend that there are major ethical challenges for 'them', for 'Asians', for example on such matters as human rights. Not for us! In the contemporary jargon of international relations, the tendency to convergence is for Westerners comfortable convergence onto a Western track. I mention this at the outset as a Western problem, to flag the broader context of the relationship between cultural West and cultural East, of which in its ethical dimensions we in Australia are only a part.

But for Australia, there is an immediate and troubling dimension to this problem, which is the challenging closeness to us of the Asian habitat. It has always been there, and there is a sense in which it has always been part of our history, because it has been a kind of Australian conscience, albeit often unwelcome, on some of the great and fundamental human issues; or the irritant which challenges the conscience, now as in the late nineteenth century, on who we embrace unreservedly as fellow human beings and whose values, in consequence, we might wish to 'converge' with, and how.

Asians are not aware of Asia being an Australian conscience, of course. Nor are most Australians. But the ethical challenges for the individual Australian in Asia derive from the ethical dimension of the nation's peculiarly inescapable bond with its regional habitat.

The decade of the official discovery of Asia, the 1980s, was also the decade in which in the realm of values Australia cast itself adrift, mindfully and almost wilfully so. So it's not surprising that no one gave any thought to the ethical dimensions of what Prime Minister Hawke came to call our 'enmeshment' with Asia. I don't entirely understand why Australia went adrift in the 1980s. But it was against such a background that the struggle to bring about real engagement with Asia took place, and it was in such an environment that decisions about Asia were made. This was the ethical landscape at home, and this domestic landscape is actually of greater importance to how we handle ourselves in Asia than what supposed tricks those Asians might be up to, to entrap us in ethical dilemmas. And what was happening in Australia reflected a doctrine of the material self, of which several elements are relevant to this subject.

One was leadership. I don't know that anyone has analysed satisfactorily the effects on society of what happened in Australian politics in late 1975. I think it encouraged a kind of cynicism, on the part both of those who approved and of those who disapproved of the actions of John Kerr and Malcolm Fraser. And perhaps something more. An Australian accountant visited me in Beijing a few months after the sacking of Whitlam, and having been all the time in China I asked him what effect he thought it had had on Australia, and he answered that he thought it had induced a widespread attitude of 'go for what you can get and bugger the morality and bugger anyone else's interests'. He had come from a conference of three or four hundred Australian accountants in Hong Kong, who had met to discuss business in Asia, and he said the discussion was pervaded by attitudes of cynicism, selfishness and greed. The talk in the coffee breaks and the corridors was all of schemes and of scams and of how to get the best out of them for your clients and for yourself. He may have been simplistic about the cause, but he was certainly prophetic.

You can't say there was no political leadership at all in the 1980s, or that it was a sole cause of what happened in business. But it was not apparent that the leadership was concerned with moral issues or with the examination of values or with much self-examination of any kind. The republican issue—profoundly about values—is something we might have debated in the 1980s, and many people expected it. That we did not may have been good or perhaps 'clever' politics. But perhaps that was the defining quality of leadership in the 1980s: 'clever politics'.

The point about politics in those years wasn't just that it made heroes out of the champions of business sleaze. Politics applauded the idea that everyone should go for the 'get-rich-quick', the material jackpot that was to come from luck or dexterity or being clever. Politics was supremely about self, and what you could get out of the society and not markedly about what you could put into it. Leadership politics in the 1980s also largely was about this.

I worked with Australian companies in Asia throughout the decade, and I have to say that one of the greatest causes of failure was the El Dorado mentality that pervaded the leadership of even some of the most conservative of Australian corporations: in for the short haul, the quick return, the profit jackpot, make a decision to go in but make another decision within less than a year to pull out because the spoils were said to be there for the picking in North America, or somewhere.

This leadership phenomenon was to have significant impact on the nature of our engagement with Asia.

The 1980s was also the decade of multiculturalism. There had been a moment, in the late 1970s, when the ending of the Vietnam War, East Timor, the new relationship with China, the boat people, and a dim awareness of how important Japan had become to us economically, produced some concentration of Australian attention on its Asian neighbours and on what manner of society we were, or wanted to be, in this neighbourhood. Multiculturalism turned the discussion of identity inwards upon itself, and it developed in what was an unforeseen and I believe entirely negative direction. By the mid–1980s, the doctrinaire end of the spectrum, the dogma that was the 'ism' on the end of 'multicultural', had developed into competitive ethnocentricism in which, as discussed in Chapter 5, identity was a matter not of what one had in common but of what distinguished one from other people living in the same country. This approach to identity often had very little to do with Australia and even disparaged Australia, and its effects were felt well beyond the communities of recent immigrants. It was narrowly self-interested, it was promoted fiercely by some representatives of ethnic communities, and it was politically encouraged. It was a reinforcing element in the doctrine of the material self, and it made it very difficult to get a clear focus on the challenges for Australia of the coming of Asia.

I chaired the Committee to Advise on Australia's Immigration Policies which delivered a report to the government in May 1988.[27] It was not the politics of the multiculturalism officials which was depressing, although they were bad enough, and devious. It was not even the secret report they prepared for the Prime Minister, which I am not supposed to have read but which is the most mendacious document I have seen in all my dealings in and with government. It was the daily fare, in the many months of hearings which preceded the writing of the report, of disparagement of Australia as having no culture, as never having had any sense of family or family values, of being overall an entirely worthless place. The companion to this lament was often lack of concern for the interests of immigrant communities other than one's own.

Separatism was never far from the representations, and the concept of community seldom meant the Australian community. They were not Australian voters but 'ethnic' voters, or the such-and-such ethnic community. Politicians fell and still fall for this, as though communities vote *en bloc* and on command from their representatives. At the more extreme end, there were ethnic community leaders who sought separate courts to operate under a separate legal and judicial regime within Australia.

Australian politicians had introduced something deeply divisive in their encouragement—not of immigration or a multicultural society, in both of which Australia ought to rejoice—but of the sectional and selfish and anti-community attitudes which were identified with the 'ism' on the end of 'multicultural'. But promote it they did. I still wonder if they even understood what was going on.

A third element of the 1980s which is of interest is what happened in education, both in schools and in the universities. Educational institutions provided very little in the way of public leadership over this period. If student demonstrations and academic strikes reflect the preoccupations of students and academics, it may be relevant that to the extent that these occurred at all in the 1980s they tended to be about money, terms and conditions of employment, fees, and other material concerns.

When it came to Asia, while there were individual academics who strove to maintain public discussion—people like Jamie Mackie and John Legge, Wang Gungwu, Nancy Viviani, John Ingleson, Colin Mackerras—the institutions themselves did not lead the charge into Asia. They followed. And this was not for some national or institutional vision or intellectual engagement or sense of commitment to the strengthening of important values of this society in the face of the challenging Asian habitat. They went for the money. And the charge was led by people who had no knowledge of or intellectual interest in the societies they visited. They established a fine reputation for Australian universities as the carpetbaggers, the gold-diggers, the mercenaries of education, a reputation which was only and with great difficulty brought under control at the end of the decade.

At the same time, in schools there emerged the phenomenon of social education referred to in Chapter 5, a kind of 'level playing field' of education in which intellectual achievement, knowledge and the discussion of values are levelled down to the capacity of the slowest mind in the education bureaucracy. By the end of the decade social education had been planted to a greater or lesser extent in all the public education systems across Australia. In its complete application (and for those curious to know what might be happening to or in store for the education of our children this is richly illustrated in a Draft Syllabus for the years from Kindergarten to the end of High School in Queensland, circulated to schools in 1992 and without ministerial knowledge or approval promoted by public servants within the Queensland Department of Education as having been approved for implementation) it proposes the abolition of the disciplines of History and Geography and any other Social Science; the homogenisation of all learning in the social sciences and much of the humanities into one subject; the elimination of study in depth of anything, to cater for the alleged inability of some students to study anything in depth; the equalising of different cultures and value systems; and the replacement of all the discipline-related experience and investigative methods and analytical approaches evolved with the accumulated contribution of some of the greatest intellects in history into one single method of investigative enquiry devised by education bureaucrats whose intellectual contribution to anything has yet to be discovered.

The social education movement was relevant on two fronts. First, to the extent that it advances, in-depth study retreats. This makes it impossible to have deep study of the societies in Asia which we do not know but which are important to our future. Second, the avoidance of deep study of Asian societies, when combined with the teaching that all cultures are to be valued equally, makes it difficult for the next generation, the people who will have to carry Australia into new and more intimate relationships with Asian cultures, to understand and analyse difference, and different values, and how we should approach them in our own dealings with the Asian region.

That is the Australian context. It was the domestic landscape for what has been possibly the most important decade in the history of Australia's relations with the outside world. Let me now try to put into it the Australian response to Asia.

The Australian discovery of Asia was dominated by institutional engagement: Commonwealth and State governments, political parties, government departments, business corporations, university administrations, media organisations. This may seem to be no more than the obvious about contemporary international relations, but it has special point when there is so little history of significant prior engagement. For Australia, not just with one country but with a whole region, there was no prior social interaction, no underpinning fabric of personal connection, no academy, no coterie of intellectuals, no community of writers or creative or performing artists; and therefore no milieu for the *mutual* discovery and exploration by individuals of such things as values, ethical issues, the place in society of the individual, matters of belief. And the problem was greatly compounded by the fact that most Australians had nothing of Asia in their formal education, and when they came to it they came without knowledge or information or intellectual preparation. This makes the nature of the institutional discovery of Asia of great interest.

As I said at the outset, my observation of the Australian institutional discovery of Asia is that, with notable exceptions, it has not only been uninformed by education or knowledge but it has been and remains largely unintellectual and unthinking, lacking in clear conceptualisation, and devoid of anything which looks far into the future—long-term thinking about ends or goals or possible outcomes not to our liking, long-term planning, long-term conceptual and operational frameworks. There was of course almost no discussion of ideals, beliefs, vision or values. Ours, not theirs.

While the reasons for Australian success and failure in Asia have barely been researched, the anecdotal evidence supports the view that Australian business in the 1980s approached Asia in a highly undifferentiated way. Most Australian companies 'had a bit of a go at Asia' in the early 1980s, and most were unsuccessful. Whether they regarded it as hard or easy, they tended to see the challenge in one Asian country as being much the same as in another. This may account in part for the widespread Australian practice of trying one Asian market and when nothing transpired after three or six or twelve months abandoning that market and trying another and then another.

Given the lack of hard knowledge and hard cultural under-standing of Asian societies bestowed on Australian business people by their formal education, it can be said that it is testimony to their business acumen that Australia has done as well as it has in business with Asia without this knowledge and understanding. To many Australians this proves that busi-ness gets done irrespective of local knowledge and skills. That attitude may have served Australia in the more distant past. It did not serve it well in the 1980s. And for the future, as the going gets tougher and even accepting that some business will always be done, the edge will belong to those who have the skills to manipulate the local market environment to their advantage.

An engagement with Asia which is simply a succession of waves of collective enthusiasm, without thought, without con-text, dominated by short-term material goals, is not conducive to the collective contemplation of ethical issues, still less to the *mutual* exploration of such issues with Asian partners. Business was not interested in such matters and never discussed them. And lacking anything much in the way of a compass, the bandwagon of enthusiasm also had a tendency to career off course. It actually rolled us backwards in the case of Indonesia, to a point where the institutional response of government and corporate Australia to Indonesia became irrational and severely damaging to our national, including our economic, interests. It then began rolling forward in that country with a momentum which could have carried us to the kind of extreme we had with China in the mid–1980s (see Chapter 2), except that China itself seems to have replaced it again.

The fundamental ethical issue for Australia—for the survival and strengthening of our society as we know it now, for the coexistence or harmonising of different ethical and value systems, for the individual Australian who will be involved increasingly in a world without borders—is not how much money we can make out of our engagement with Asia, or what to do when someone holding public office wants a bribe. It is to cast our minds forward, say 50 years, to a time when we are totally cheek by jowl with our Asian neighbours, when every facet of Australian life, from entertainment to industrial relations to political party platforms, will be affected by Asian societies and cultures. It is to ask ourselves: what forces will dominate Australia? whose political ideals? whose principles and values? And the very long term may give us some different ideas about the long term, and where we can temporise and where we should stand firm, who we placate and where that will lead us.

It is this question, of where we think we will stand, or be able to stand, on ethical issues 30 years hence, which is the most important ethical dimension of our engagement with Asia now. And the question must be addressed and publicly debated. There also has to be some shared exploration with Asian societies of our respective ideals and beliefs and codes of ethics, some mutuality about how we handle different ideas about ethics as we move closer together.

Because there is now this discussion across the Asian region about similar matters. It has its wellspring in many issues and in widely differing parts of the political spectrum. It is expressed as a concern about the erosion of what are described as 'traditional' values and the family, about the breakdown of social cohesion, about decline in moral standards, about greed and lack of accountability and the absence of spirituality among the young. These may be the woes of modernisation, but they are quite often laid at the door of the West.

In a related development, in late 1992 in Kuala Lumpur a group of intellectuals drawn from most countries in East Asia, and India and Bangladesh, thinkers actively engaged in public policy debate in their own countries, established a forum called the Commission for a New Asia. This commission met several times, and attempted to establish a framework for discussion of these issues of beliefs, principles, and codes of ethics, and to explore the potential for what might be called an Asian 'New Asia', one not obliterated by Western culture and values.[28] These people are not an anti-human rights brigade. Still less were they anti-Western. Maybe slightly conservative, but radical enough to agree to a joint statement of beliefs which includes one that revolution is justified when oppression becomes unbearable.

There were several things which were important about the work of this commission. One was that it was engaged in a process of identifying values, principles and ethical positions which Asian societies have *in common*. Fashionable thinking in Western societies is that there no single Asia. This is true, and a necessary corrective to earlier stereotyping which lumps Japanese with Javanese and cannot tell the difference. But fashionable thinking is also tending to an extreme position which sees nothing in common between Asian societies, and holds, for example, that there is no single 'Asian' approach to anything, including ethics. In one sense this may be true because ethical differences derive in such large part from cultural differences, and in any event ethical positions tend to change with the social and economic evolution of society. But I wonder also if it does not suit Westerners to believe that Asian societies have nothing in common. There is also the problem that the research that has been conducted on ethics has been almost entirely from a Western perspective.[29] The work of this commission made remarkable progress on establishing common ground between people from very disparate cultural backgrounds.

The other aspect of the commission's work which is important to this discussion was its reflection on contemporary Western values as projected in Asia. While recognising and welcoming the great Western inheritance which is the free and open democratic society in which there is respect for the individual and for human rights, the discussions of the commission drew on Asian views which reflect a rather different perception of Western *practice* in Asia. The perception is that Western practice, far from being ethical, is often arbitrary, hypocritical and shot through with double standards, that it is more about imposing than converging, that it assaults traditional values and debases culture.

I think this may come as a surprise to many Australians who go to Asia for business or government or the universities. In a major three-year project under the title Australian–Asian Perceptions, the Academy of Social Sciences in Australia produced a study, *Perceiving Business Ethics*, published jointly with the Asia–Australia Institute. This study reports that the comments of Australians on business in Asia project an impression that Asian business people are dishonest, devious and corrupt, while Australian business people are far from having such tendencies! The same study also cites a survey by Professor Robert Armstrong which identifies ten types of ethical problems which worry Australian executives: small-scale bribery, large-scale bribery, gifts/favours/entertainment, pricing, product and technology abuses, tax evasion practices, illegal/immoral activities in the host country, questionable commission deals, cultural differences, involvement in political affairs.[30] Issues relating to the abuse of human rights, by the way, seem not to be on the list of concerns of Australian business executives.

The study goes on, however, to cite a number of areas in which Australians might be considered corrupt and Asians ethical, or where Asians have a very clear commitment to ethical positions in business practice which are measured by different standards from Western ones, or where what we condemn in Asian societies is widely practised at home. A survey was cited, for example, which showed that one-third of New South Wales public servants thought that appointing a colleague to a job without advertising it, or using their position to get a friend a job, was not corrupt.[31]

Which brings me back to where I started. My view of this issue—the ethical dimensions of our engagement with Asian countries—is that it challenges us to examine our own position rather than to pass judgment on others. And it seems to me that nationally it is we who have the problem. I am not suggesting for a moment that other countries in the region do not have problems, and I am not unconcerned for the problems of the individual business person faced with corruption or the flouting by business counterparts of their own laws or of what we might regard as ethical standards. And I happen to be an Australian who would not want to swap my society for any other in the region, or to see us abandon the principles and values on which it is founded and which I think we need fiercely to defend.

But on this issue we have a problem, which consists in several matters:

1   We started in Asia with a supposition of moral and ethical superiority, which often cannot be justified.

2   We entered into a close engagement with Asia over a decade characterised domestically by a relative absence of concern for moral or ethical standards of behaviour, on a national scale.

3   This close engagement is dominated by institutions driven by short-term material goals, and there is still no leader in public life who has attended to the matter of where today's decisions will leave us in 50 or even 30 years' time.

4   We believe that if there are lapses in ethical behaviour these are on the part of Asians, and that our only ethical problem, in all our righteousness, is how to cope with the terrible decisions with which this confronts us.

5   We contend that the longer-term solution is for Asian countries to adopt our codes of ethical behaviour—shaky *in practice* though some of these may have been shown to be or to have become—through a process of convergence, which there is no way we can conceive of as being anything other than onto our track.

6   To the idea that there may be values or ethical codes in Asia which could with benefit to us be incorporated into our value systems we respond with reactions ranging from cultural stereotyping of the worst kind to smirking self-righteousness.

For a country which acknowledges a future inextricably bound up with Asia—1990s style as partners and equals, not 1890s style as Social Darwinists let loose in Asia's southern hemisphere—all this presents a problem.

How are we to move forward? In a prize-winning article in the *Harvard Business Review* in 1987, Sir Adrian Cadbury makes the point that 'There is no simple, universal formula for solving ethical problems. We have to choose from our own codes of conduct whichever rules are appropriate to the case in hand; the outcome of those choices makes us who we are'.[32] I have run a consulting practice for Australian clients since 1978, and I have worked with over 200 Australian companies and government agencies, mainly in China but also in Korea, Taiwan,

Japan, Indonesia and other parts of Asia. And I know the choices are not easy. Leaving aside the dilemma that as consultant you are not the one who makes the decisions on these matters (and that the kind of choice you often face is whether it is ethical to abandon a client when your own ethical beliefs demand that you should, or walk away from business which would associate you with something you can't condone), the real problem is that most Australians don't seem to have much consciousness of ethical issues, or at least don't seem to have any kind of coherent thinking about codes of conduct to help them through the decisions.

The Academy of the Social Sciences' suggestion is that the complexity of the business ethics issue in Asia is such that we need an ethical framework; that is, a framework of general principles of ethical action from which standards of business behaviour can be derived. I think that is certainly pointing in the right direction, but it also goes to the heart of the much larger issues I have touched on earlier. Because the problem for the business person is not in isolation. It needs a broad Australian context, and a deep understanding of the broad Asian context, and a very long-term perspective on where we think we want Australian society to end up, as close partners in a political confederation where the weight of numbers will be Asian. And identity. I am not one who believes in a fixed and single Australian identity. But to those who ask why we are always agonising about what is our identity I say that we have to know ourselves if we are to know how to move in the challenging environment of Asia and to hold to the things we love about this society.

This is why I am concerned with political leadership. And with what is fundamental to the Australian identity and the Australian polity rather than the jostling over ethnicity which passes for discussion of how we identify as Australian and what we have in common. And with what goes on in our education systems. Because I think we let ourselves down badly on all three fronts in the 1980s.

But we now have a chance to build on the lessons of that decade. Let us work on a framework, but a framework of a larger kind, from which not only business but government people and academics and everyone else will be able to draw ideas and inspiration for working through the ethical issues of their engagements with Asian countries.

The first requirement is to debate and develop perspectives

on what we want for Australian society 30 years hence, perspectives which are not cast in or determined only in economic terms. This is imperative, and urgent. We have committed ourselves to becoming part of a region of which we have not previously been part but which is overwhelmingly culturally different. And for many reasons that process is now irreversible.

But second, let us not proceed as though we can work it out in isolation from the regional habitat. We need to establish ourselves in a forum or forums with Asian countries for the *shared* discussion of principles and values and beliefs and visions and morals and ethics and education. We will not need to accept their views, but we must understand them and factor them in to our long-term perspectives and perhaps modify our expectations and our behaviour to take account of them. It is in such a forum or forums also that we can develop our thinking on human rights, although I would be against attaching it to a human rights forum because of the particular sharpness and self-righteousness which often attaches to both sides in that discussion. What I am suggesting needs to be more open. And I suggest also that it should be entirely new, and not grafted onto forums which deal exclusively with economic futures.

It is in these terms that I see the issue of Asia as being about the Australian identity. Asia is already changing the Australian identity in ways which I have talked about elsewhere in this book. But here I mean it is a challenge to us to prove to ourselves that we have an identity worth preserving. We can no longer just take its preservation for granted.

It is in these terms also that I see Asia as an Australian conscience. What are the measures of our own humanity? To what extent are we really prepared to embrace Asia? Could we bring ourselves to look to Asia first, on fundamental issues? Or do we still hanker after a white man's answers and a white man's world? Could we accept some Asian modification in our thinking and behaviour, to take account of Asian values and beliefs and ethical codes? Do we grasp at convergence in the hope that they are right, the convergence theorists who say that industrial societies will converge on a similar set of characteristics, including values, now present in Europe and North America and Australia? Would we be so willing if we thought convergence was onto a track that was 'Asian'?

I don't believe we have yet made that decision about ourselves. I am a constant champion when I am in Asia for Australia and for the great success of Asian immigration and the many other things which make this a lovely, honey-coloured society. But consciously, intellectually, in relation to ourselves and the real Asia that is out there, I don't believe that as a nation we have yet made that commitment. And that, perhaps, is the greatest ethical issue for us all.

CHAPTER 9

A Chinese world

I put this question to a group of Australian executives in 1996 and not one of them got it right: what is Sime Darby? Sime Darby happens to be the largest company in Malaysia, 85 years old, with a market capitalisation of over US$6 billion, a multinational conglomerate with over 200 companies in operations in 22 countries including Australia. If knowing the present is difficult, knowing the future is hard indeed. Nothing in our education or upbringing trains us to pick a time far into the future and hold it in focus and imagine it. We need something to relate to. So let me begin with some observations to help ease the mind into thinking about the long-term future.

The first is that the people we hire now in their early twenties and just starting their careers will be the managers and executives of the 2020s, 25 to 30 years hence. What kind of skills, what kind of people, will we need in these positions in 30 years' time? Can we remember 1966? Did we imagine then, in that world, a world in which there would be no Soviet Union, and the most common language of business in Asia would be Chinese, and Japan would be the biggest donor of international aid, and Asia, not the United States or Europe, the powerhouse of global economic growth, and providing most of its own investment capital, and the pacesetting Asian economies already part of the developed world, and seemingly everyone anywhere with mobile phones, and everyone every-where watching satellite television and doing something called surfing the net? Did we anticipate that future and plan for the kind of people we would need to manage it? Or did we think there was no need because the world would be pretty much the same?

What kind of skills should we require today of the people who will be our managers and executives in 30 years' time?

Another observation: the World Bank says that by the year 2020 China will have the biggest economy in the world, about 25 per cent larger than the United States, which will be in second place.[33] The British Treasury says that by 2015 China will have joined the G7.[34]

A third: by the 2020s, on current projections, the percentage of the Australian population of Asian descent will be between 7 and 10 per cent (depending on the definitions).

These are not facts, just something to help imagine the future. We have to imagine that by the 2020s almost all of the givens in the current external environment of Australia will no longer hold, because the world is just not going to be the same. This suggests that there is some hard thinking to be done about the 2020s.

Here is a view about the 2020s and the Asian region. It is one view; there are others, and this one is necessarily specula-tive. But it does start from current realities, and the sweep of history.

There is already now in train across Asia a change which is taking place on many fronts, whose effects will be greater than anything we have seen since postwar decolonisation. This change will work itself out over a time-span ranging from now forward over the next 30 years. By the end of that period the United States will not be the power in East Asia that can enforce its will. That will be China.

The two most important elements of this regional change go hand in hand: the change in power relativities across the Pacific—the power of the United States relative to East Asia—and the maturing of the phenomenon of Asianisation.

Let me begin with the United States. We look at the United States and we see it locked in confrontation with Japan, or China, and we may think this is because of the present US Administration, for example, or the unwillingness of Japan to open its economy or take a leadership role in Asia, or the refusal of the Chinese Government to bend to the US will on human rights or other issues. But these explanations conceal a fundamental issue. This is that the rise of East Asia is about power and the assertion of it, and this changing relativity in power relations between Asia and the United States. It matters not that for the moment and for some time to come the United States will remain the pre-eminent military power and a major market for all on this side of the Pacific, as well as a major source of investment, technology and ideas. The point is that there is an underlying, long-term and historic shift in power relations, with a relative decline in US power in Asia and in the US will to use its power in Asia. The outcomes of this shift will be with us for a long time to come.

The shift is evident not just in the case of Japan and China. Over the last few years, the United States has found itself in dispute, sometimes public and sometimes acrimonious, with many of its friends and partners on this side of the Pacific—notably with Japan and China, but also with Indonesia, Singapore, Malaysia, Thailand, the Philippines, Korea and Australia. These are to varying degrees all manifestations of this historic shift, wherein the once dominant partner in Asia has been wrestling with problems which arise from a development which for the most part it does not understand or even recognise. This is not easy, and it explains some of the clumsiness and inconsistency of US diplomacy in the region. The experience is difficult for the United States and often emotional. The US Government often objects angrily, for example, to any proposal from Asia for multilateral regional cooperation which excludes the United States, charging that this is 'drawing a line' down the middle of the Pacific. But it is the shift in power, if anything, which is drawing such a line and not some kind of anti-US alliance.

This comes at a time in American history when Americans are deeply troubled about the present condition of their own society, exemplified in the reaction to the Los Angeles riots in May 1992. The idea of the American Dream, for so long so sustaining, imagined a never-ending upward progression in American society. To many Americans the American Dream seems no longer to deliver the future. It comes at a time also when there has been some tendency to contraction of the global horizons of many in America—not full-blown isolationism, but a tendency in that direction. The emotional and psychological and cultural adjustment to the challenge of Asia is made more difficult by this tendency.

This domestic questioning affects the way the United States looks at the world. It often seems confused about values and beliefs. In the past it could believe it was right because it was promoting and defending 'the good' (freedom, democracy). Now, who knows what it believes? This is reflected in such matters as the handling of the most favoured nation issue with China in 1993 and 1994. Whether or not the United States should have taken the stand it did in the first place, for it then to cave in when the deadline arrived a year later on this matter of proclaimed fundamental principle was not only bad politics, worse diplomacy, and still worse principle; it was also very revealing of the changed role the United States *already* has in Asia. There have been similar contradictions in the US handling of intellectual property rights in China in 1995 and 1996.

The combination of these things accounts for the problem of US will to use its power in Asia. Under the Clinton Administration, there has been widespread scepticism in Asia about the US commitment to the region's security. The United States was lukewarm about the Philippines' concerns about Chinese actions in the South China Sea, and in some ways strong but also equivocal over the March 1996 Taiwan Straits crisis.

This does not mean that the United States is decrepit, or will become so. The contraction of its power, commitment and resolve is relative, and the relative factor across the Pacific is the emerging power, commitment and resolve in East Asia. There may indeed be a 'unipolar' world in a military sense now that the Soviet Union has gone. But the new forces across the Pacific from the United States combine to present an Asian challenge to this unipolarity, composed of several things. It is most obviously, of course, economic. Not just the economic weight and performance of Asian economies, but the economic vitality and self-confidence and independence of mind and action that flow from the performance. And the knowledge that the region now generates more than 80 per cent of its own capital and, with the rise of the Asian middle class, is creating markets which in total rival in size the middle class of the United States and which within this generation will come to exceed the entire population of the United States. No one in their right mind in the United States or the Western world can any longer patronise the economies of East Asia. On the contrary, Asian leaders from Japan to Southeast Asia believe they are in some ways superior to the United States in economic management and performance, and some of them openly express this view.

The second element of the Asian challenge is political, the challenge of political assertiveness. This is commonly seen as a product of the end of the Cold War, but that is to obscure its underlying cause. Asian governments are saying to the United States that it is not acceptable to be treated as less than equal, 'junior' partners, or children, and they have the maturity and confidence to assert it. The book *The Japan That Can Say No* was an early manifestation of this challenge, and it created a furore in Washington at the time. But why should it? If we think about it, why should not Japan, or anyone else in Asia, be able to say 'No' to Washington? In any event, across the region now, Asians and Asian governments are saying 'No'.[35] China says 'No' on human rights, but so does Indonesia say 'No' on a variety of issues, and Singapore, and many others. In 1995 Thailand said 'No' to the United States on its proposal for a new military deployment or small permanent cell in that country. So for the first time, the United States is faced with an array of independent countries in Asia which are successfully standing up to it on many fronts, politically, not militarily, but sometimes in tacit cooperation with each other. But it is *not* anti-American.

The third element of the Asian challenge is the challenge of culture, not in the sense of the assertion of Asian culture and values but what we might call the challenge *to* culture, American culture, in the broadest sense of the term. American culture is under challenge at home from the penetration of talented and cross-culturally adept Asian individuals. In education, for example, top places and some top schools in the United States are dominated and even monopolised by Asian students. But it is in every other aspect of American society, from the concert hall to the science laboratory and even in the appearance of Asian faces on television and the sporting field. Thirty years ago this would have been unthinkable. Many Americans find it very exciting, but in a society disturbed by the external challenge of Asia this internal challenge can also be confusing, even unwelcome.

In some way, of course, this is also the challenge of ethnicity, a challenge to the West in general, not in the way of Genghis Khan in Europe, but as the final act in the centuries-long drama of Western domination of Asia, and the challengers are not 'hordes' or armies but individuals. It is individual challenge, by outstanding performance of Asian individuals in things which Americans value, and hold to be very much their own.

Where is this leading, the US decline and the Asian challenge? I am not in any sense suggesting a future in which the United States is 'finished'. But already, whatever happens in East Asia affects the United States. It used to be the other way round. So what we have is a change not just in economic relativities but in the balance of influence and hence also in the balance of political power.

This will continue into the future, and by the mid–2020s the weight of political power and influence will lie with East Asia. It will no longer be a place in which the United States is the determining power. The implications for all are enormous. The United States will be a partner and player, and a major one, and a welcome one. But also, I would suggest, only when it is an invited one. And the countries of East Asia are already anticipating this. APEC is of interest here. Whatever the motivations may be now, I think APEC will come to be seen as the region's collective recognition that the United States is diminishing in power and influence, and also in will. It is a collective determination that the United States should not withdraw to its side of the Pacific and put up the shutters but should remain, engaged but changed, as an important and valued partner, indispensable to the attainment of open regionalism and free trade, and a necessary counterweight to other regional players at a time of great historic transition.

This change is occurring at the same time as Asian leaders are becoming increasingly conscious about Asian culture and Asian values, and of common ground, common perspectives, common ways of looking at themselves and their future and at Western society, and a common determination to try to avoid going the way of the West in its social breakdown and degradation. This is the precursor to the emergence some time between now and the 2020s, but almost certainly earlier rather than later, of the Asian Community I have spoken of, confined to this side of the Pacific.

It is not yet clear whether this Community will have an ideological dimension, in which an idea of what Asia stands for is distinguished from an idea of what the West stands for, but there is already some myth-making about it in Asia. Some of this contends that shared regional culture and values are Confucian culture and values. There is an enormous amount of rubbish claimed on behalf of Confucian culture, and a tendency to romanticise, idealise and mythologise 'Confucian' societies (China, including Hong Kong and Taiwan, Japan, Korea, Singapore, Vietnam) and to suggest that some values are exclusive to these societies. But values relating to the family, and hierarchy, and harmony, are present in other, 'non-Confucian', Asian societies; so also hard work, thrift, and respect for learning. They may exist in different mix, but they are there.

The mythologising of the history and culture and values of Asian societies is not, however, confined to Confucianists. It is more widespread. It is ahistorical. And it contains some dangers, because there are some signs that the emerging Asian 'Asia' could go the way the West did and make such myths about itself that it comes to believe it is the ultimate and only repository of virtue and good behaviour. In some quarters this already has the flavour of political orthodoxy. But a united Asian region driven by such political orthodoxy is a united region to be feared, and for Australia it is critically important that we work for the maintenance of regional pluralism as the guarantee of heterodoxy and independence.

The essential message for Australia is that, by the 2020s and almost certainly long before, the dominant influences in the region will be countries and governments whose outlook and values derive from cultures very different from our own. That is what is important about ASEM, and Australia's position on APEC. We assumed no countervailing development on the Western side of the Pacific, and no change in the relativities of US power. But if we anticipate a region shaped and influenced by Asian societies and cultures, this should mean not that we abandon APEC but that we stop belittling other ideas and try to join and share in what is happening separately in Asia, so that we can be part of it when it comes and not just subject to it.

CHINA AS THE DOMINANT POWER

We can argue about who will be dominant in East Asia, but all the indications are that it will be China. Economic projections suggest it; some military projections do the same. Already the countries of East Asia are treading gingerly around China and its sensitivities. This does not mean they like or dislike China. They simply recognise the power and the potential to project it. An Indonesian minister said to me recently that we have to work out how to prevent the rest of the countries in Asia from becoming simply China's special economic zones. Even with the most benign of governments in Beijing, Chinese power will be felt throughout the region. I do not ignore Japan or Indonesia, or Korea or Malaysia, all of which will be important and powerful. But China will dominate.

There are some who think China will not make it, that ethnic separatism, inequalities, population growth and other problems will produce chaotic conditions, disintegration and civil wars. There are still those who fear a return to a kind of Maoist China.

Chinese politics is of course unstable. It could fall apart. The Chinese Communist Party has lost it, the Party itself and all it goes by in the way of ideological conformity, statewide control, 'commandism' from the centre. No one believes in it. The Party remains, but there is still nothing to put in its place. At the same time international communism is also laid bare in all its evils, and discredited. Even if someone wanted to reassert that kind of control in China, it could not do so because the Party is not now dealing with an exhausted, cowed and desperately poor populace. We have to remember that the Party came to power in 1949 because the people turned to it for salvation. Few would do that now, although many are joining it as a path to position and preferment. And the Party in the old sense has lost its will. This does not mean that they don't try to control what people read and think, or put people in gaol, violate human rights every day, maintain files on everyone, and control intellectuals and political opponents. But China did all of that before the communists, and so did Taiwan until the 1970s, and so still to some extent do Korea and Singapore. Many Chinese in fact approved of the putting down of the demonstrations in Beijing in June 1989, and many of those I hear this from are in Taiwan and Singapore.

There is no doubt that China also has massive problems elsewhere, including regional disparities in wealth, a huge itinerant population, and the overwhelming burden of inefficient and insolvent state enterprises. There are, however, more factors in the equation which suggest that China is going to make it than there is evidence of eventual collapse, Soviet-style, and these include the following.

One is China's track record. It is now twenty years since Mao died, and there has been rather extraordinary effective economic and political management over the period. Extraordi-

nary, because this has been management of change on a huge
scale, management of a transition few others in history have
confronted and from a tradition no other country has had to
bear. They have managed—to take a few examples at random—
the dismantling of communal agriculture and wholesale agri-
cultural reform, the introduction of a modern education system,
the dismantling of the irrational socialist pricing structure, the
establishment of a realistic exchange rate, the opening of industry to foreign participation, the development of consumerism
including department stores and chains selling made-outside-
China goods direct to the Chinese consumer, the application to
just about every part of China—including Tibet!—of special
economic zone policies trialled with such success in Shenzhen,
the employment-generating effects of investment from off-shore,
and the policy that the free market rules (with a last nostalgic
nod in the direction of Chairman Mao by calling it market
socialism). All this, and much more.

And it has worked well enough for China to be a magnet
for international investment. Two major and many minor political eruptions in the streets have neither brought the regime
down nor turned it from its purpose. China is of course not
democratic. But perhaps you have to have lived in China before
to know just how open it is now, and how many people have
a sense of freedom about their lives and their ability to come
and go and do as they please.

A second factor has been the role of Chinese tycoons, at
first from Hong Kong but later from Southeast Asia and Taiwan.
Their knowledge and experience and advice has been and still
is at the direct service of Chinese leaders, and has guided and
will continue to guide the leadership through many difficult
decisions of economic reform and liberalisation in an informal
and private way.

A third is the resumption of what might be called traditional Chinese politics. One part of this is the restoration in
party and government of rule by great families and their
extended connections and family alliances. Most Chinese of
course prefer that government stay as far away from them as
possible. However, they also recognise that it is a fact of life
that governments almost by definition continually make trouble, not only through taxes and other impositions (hence the
well-known and universal practice in Taiwan whereby every
business has two sets of books), but by their internal disputes
and conflicts, and civil wars and warlordism of the kind seen

in the first half of this century. They have therefore learnt to accept political instability as an ever-imminent possibility, and to live with it and through it. They would never have made the mistake Western leaders made about the way in which the Chinese Government handled Tiananmen because they would not have expected otherwise. But the re-emergence of rule by great families ties government back into a very familiar relationship with society, and business, which everyone knows and feels more or less comfortable with. Chinese societies live by such connections, and their restoration at the top and throughout the provinces restores the networks which communicate and facilitate and cushion. The families which rule Beijing all have strong ties with business interests and tycoons, inside China, in Hong Kong and Macao and Southeast Asia, and in Taiwan.

Another feature of traditional Chinese politics is the general acceptance in such societies of what is called 'power distance', which accords rulers and leaders much greater freedom to pursue and enjoy power and its rewards than in English-speaking societies. Although this may change over time, for the foreseeable future it will mitigate the tensions between the haves in power and the have-nots. The Chinese Government understands that there is a limit to public tolerance of the use of office for personal gain, and applies brakes to keep it in acceptable bounds.

A fourth factor is that Chinese are almost by birth or instinct materialist. In Chinese society anywhere that is the hallmark. You have to have money to satisfy that instinct, and no people I know work harder at making money if they are allowed to keep it than Chinese. In that once purest of Marxist-Leninist countries, Chinese are now allowed to do both. Ideology is out. Getting rich is in. Unless you live next door to a jealous official who hasn't had the opportunity to line his pockets, there are no inhibitions on legitimately making money and getting rich. So the Chinese are now in their natural element, and revelling in it. Disposable incomes are rising. And so is the size of the middle class. In one sense—aspiration— every Chinese is born middle-class. In terms of more conventional measurements of what is middle-class, its size is already somewhere between 2 and 5 per cent of the total population, probably already around 30 million people and rising fast. These are concentrated in the southern and coastal provinces. Pursuit of the material, and getting rich, is a 'freedom'. This is now open to everyone to seek (even if they don't all find), and everyone in the political process is benefiting materially in some way or other. Many of course have their snouts deep in the trough. Every ministry and department and bureau and provincial government and research institute in China, and almost every one of the powerful personalities, has an office or corporation or some beneficial connection in Shenzhen, Hong Kong or somewhere where the money action is, and many have children studying abroad. Political instability of any kind will be detrimental to these interests. But there are many more who benefit simply from companies in which they have a legitimate interest, or from the general rewards available to the middle class in a growth economy.

A fifth factor is that element of the Chinese tradition which emphasises hard work. In combination with luck, this is the formula for getting rich. There has to be some connection of course between hard work and reward, and in the state enterprises where there is little or no reward, hard work is less evident. But for the rest, the rewards are driving the hard work which is making China the engine of growth in East Asia.

Sixth, and the secret weapon in China's economic development, is Chinese outside China—not just the tycoons, but the vast numbers from Southeast Asia and Taiwan and Hong Kong, and North America and Australia. This is sometimes referred to as 'Greater China', a politically difficult term because it frightens many in Asia, particularly non-Chinese Southeast Asians, by any of the definitions attaching to its use. One definition is ethnic and cultural, and it includes just about everyone in Asia who is Chinese, or who identifies as Chinese. Another is political. It refers to Taiwan, Hong Kong and the Chinese mainland, and is a way of getting around Beijing's extreme sensitivity to calling these three entities the 'Three Chinas'. And one is almost purely economic, and means the Chinese mainland, Hong Kong and Taiwan, but also Macao and the Chinese people in other parts of Asia who are involved economically with China, Hong Kong and Taiwan. The population of the mainland is about 1.2 billion. Hong Kong is over 6 million, and Taiwan 21 million. But there are another 30 million Chinese spread throughout Asia, from Korea in the north to Indonesia in the south.

No other developing country in history has had such a fantastic advantage as China in this regard, not even Israel. And it's not just that there are lots of Chinese. It's that they also happen to control much of the banking and finance and commerce in Indonesia, Singapore, Malaysia, Thailand, the Philippines and of course Hong Kong. And they control the whole of Taiwan, which has the world's largest foreign currency reserves, and is chock-full of the technology China needs, and people to transfer it who have been trained in the best colleges and universities in the United States, and yet who need no middleman to facilitate with language or cultural familiarity. These Chinese investors started with small-scale investments. They are now involved in major investments in energy, infrastructure, construction—and everything else including department stores.

The multiplier effects of this input are felt not only on the Chinese mainland but in Taiwan and Hong Kong as well. In combination they are creating a new economic phenomenon whose dynamism and generative capacity I think few Westerners can understand or even conceive of. This is the coming of the age of modern China, and it is apparent in a new sense of confidence among Chinese in all parts of Asia, and even a degree of assertiveness, a kind of 'coming out' from the background in which repressive policies in a number of Southeast Asian countries had kept them.

The *modus operandi* of Chinese business is connections. Family connections, clan connections, state of origin connections, school connections, and where there are none of those, simply other Chinese. With the benefit of these connections, they are setting about making a kind of Chinese industrial revolution, with southern China increasingly the furnace. For example, Chinese in Taiwan and Singapore and Bangkok are jumping onto planes bound for Vietnam, where, of course, Chinese used to control much of the financial and economic life. In Thailand, whose business and banking is still controlled largely by Sino-Thais, new highways will link northern Thailand to the Vietnamese coast. Notwithstanding the differences which still exist between Vietnam and China, that border will ultimately cease to exist economically and commercially. Regional Chinese airlines—there are now about 30—are already flying into Bangkok and Kuala Lumpur and Singapore. And the linking up of southern China and the economies of Thailand and Vietnam and the financial and business empires of Singapore and Indonesia and Malaysia is creating a firestorm of economic activity in southern China, which defies the retardants of poverty and population and the after-effects of 40 years of socialism, and not only fuels the economic development of China but will expand its geographical scope and create the most powerful economic force in Asia. Already, cross-national investment in Asia by Chinese exceeds that of Japan.

Investment capital, people, technology and knowhow are pouring into China from these sources. Every time China should by all logic at least falter, there is this continuing infusion of strength from Chinese overseas.

A seventh factor is that the Chinese system itself has evolved, since the passing of the Mao era, into a kind of Chinese federalism. This cushions the tensions between the centre and the provinces, and distributes powers and functions in a more satisfactory way. Some of the provinces are already strong enough not to want further independence from Beijing. They can thumb their noses at the centre if it seeks to use the state for other than sensible policy, strategic and functional responsibilities of national government. The centre knows that for economic reasons alone China cannot be allowed to dismember itself, and the provinces recognise that there is economic benefit in being together. The politics of federalism are difficult to manage, but the brokering role of the central government is critical to all the provincial players, and the web of family and personal relationships assists greatly in tying it all together. I see little sign here that China is disintegrating.

The eighth and in some ways the most potent factor is the Chinese nationalism which is now hardening across the country. Some in the West see the newly strident nationalism as being simply the manufactured product of official policy, giving people something to believe in now that communism is dead. It may be that too, but it is more spontaneous and it is deeply grassroots. It is also fanned by US policies and actions. Each time the United States pushes China, even on such matters as the protection of intellectual property, this nationalism becomes more widespread, more conscious and more explicit. I do not know how far this is understood in Washington, but US China policy is now the single most potent force driving a chauvinistic nationalism of a kind not seen in China since Mao's time. It is strongly cultural and in some quarters quite xenophobic. It equates current US China policies with 150 years of Western depredations in China. Nationalism in turn reinforces Chinese collectivist solidarity. Chinese may quarrel among themselves, as different ingroups. Against the outside world, it is the Chinese ingroup which comes first. Chinese group nationalism is now hitched to China's economic growth and influence and China's sense of having arrived to take its place in the world. The bid for the 2000 Olympics revealed many things about China. What was most revealing for all of us who live in the East Asian region was that the Chinese believed that the 2000 games were theirs, as of right, simply because they had applied, not because they had the best bid. Many Chinese believe they lost only because of US opposition. I have even had Chinese officials say to me that Australia 'stole' the games from China, which also says something about a Chinese perception of Australia's relations with the United States.

When the above factors are added together, I think there can be no doubt that China *is* going to make it. Between now and 2020, China's influence will begin to permeate the region and Australian society in ways which we have only known previously with Britain and the United States. Its influence on us will be intermixed with that of Japan, and Indonesia, and other major players, and this will compound our problems of adjustment, even if it also offers us some balancing options. But the overwhelming influence will be that of China. Over this period also, East Asia will come together more formally in an East Asia Community. But it will be China which will dominate it, and China will run it if the other participants are not thoughtful and far-sighted enough to make arrangements which will produce a more diffused distribution of influence. China went to ASEM. It attends all the major regional conclaves. But it is still seen by its neighbours as not yet fully engaged in these forums. This may be because it does not yet see its way clear to getting its own way.

CITY-STATES AND CITY-REGIONS IN EAST ASIA'S FUTURE

There is one aspect of China's regional role in an East Asian Community which offers some interesting possibilities, and which warrants digression into the matter of Hong Kong. The constituents of an East Asian Community are generally thought of as only the nation-states of the region, but this need not be so. There is a relatively recent development in East Asia which could make for different kinds of membership, or at least a sub-layer of smaller and relatively independent constituents in such a Community. This is the redrawing of economic boundaries, and the creation of new economic sub-regions within states, city-regions, growth triangles which cross national borders (for example between Singapore, Malaysia and Indonesia) and broader sub-regions (as between Taiwan, Hong Kong and Guandong Province). There is some similarity between those which cross national borders and those within one country, for example in China, where growth sub-regions are emerging in many parts of the country. Singapore is developing another model, which is the Singapore off-shore special zone, of which there is one in Suzhou in the Chinese province of Jiangsu. These are a kind of Singapore-sponsored satellite economy, in another country, by invitation and without the colonialism which went with earlier European examples in Asia.

The Asian region still has a long way to go in the evolution of these regions, but it is already apparent that they can assume an importance as entities in their own right, defined not only by economic flows but by tariff and other rules and their own distinctive internal commercial and investment environment. Hong Kong and South China are dramatic examples. These entities by and large ignore political boundaries. And in an only slightly tongue-in-cheek vision of how this phenomenon might develop, Singapore Minister for Information and the Arts George Yeo has suggested the possibility of these becoming not only the characteristic form of economic entity in Asia, but joined to each other in some modern, twenty-first-century Asian version of the thirteenth-century north European Hanseatic League. Hong Kong would be an obvious candidate for participation in this 'Asian Hanseatic League'. Once the tension between the Chinese government and the British colonial presence is removed, a variety of scenarios will be available to Hong Kong, just as they are already to other parts of China. It should become possible to think about a Hong Kong in an East Asian region made up of both national states and economic city-regions which ignore the political boundaries of nation-states. This would give Hong Kong a great opportunity to capitalise on those things which have made it strong.

I spent the formative years of learning about Asia in Hong Kong, and have lived there again since, and visit often. When I first lived in Hong Kong, one of the things that struck me was what I would now describe as its Asia-wide awareness and outlook. To some extent it had to be, because its life was then, as Richard Hughes wrote, a matter of 'borrowed place, borrowed time',[36] and the events of the Asian region could have swept its fortunes one way or another at any moment. But as a young student and diplomat, I was educated and influenced by Hong Kong's cosmopolitan regionalism. I was surprised at the regional coverage in the local media. I went in awe of people I met at dinner, who lived in Hong Kong and traversed the region from Korea to Indonesia, and knew those countries and their leaders in business, as reporters, as engineers, or as tourists, and who were already regional in their thinking.

Hong Kong was an international city, but not in a European or North American sense. It was quintessentially of this region. It may have been ultimately part of China, but it was already—and before this could have been said of any other city in Asia—part of the Asian region. Hong Kong taught me what it was to be a citizen of the region, and I believe it is as a citizen of the region and not just as a special region of China that Hong Kong can find a special identity. This has to be worked on, and there could always be events in China which could impede such an outcome. But on balance I believe that is how it could work, because I'm an optimist about China succeeding in its economic transformation, because it's in China's interests, and because the long-term trend within China itself seems to be towards greater regional autonomy and a limited but expanding pluralism.

Hong Kong's capacities as a major city-region and hub in East Asia are perhaps greater than those of any other place in the region. The most often noted are the financial and commercial. But Hong Kong has many other capacities. One is Hong Kong people. As in many things, so on this I defer to my long-time friend, colleague and mentor, Professor Wang Gungwu.[37] He points out that Hong Kong people are distinct from Taiwanese and from Overseas Chinese. They are Hong Kong. I do not have the deep knowledge of this issue that Professor Wang has, but one point I infer from his observation is that they are not just another bunch of Cantonese. They have Cantonese characteristics of course, but they also have this background of being a sophisticated, regionally oriented community, which made and feels part of the only city in China to have been continuously and internationally commercial since the end of World War II. The people, not the city, developed as the link between the Asian region and the rest of China, between Taiwan and China, between Overseas Chinese and China, between China and Asia and between China and the rest of the world, even in the most isolated of China's days.

Some cities are without an essence and some have a distinctive essence. Hong Kong is one of the latter, and I think its essence is sophisticated regionalism, providing a regional hub for Chinese and for East Asia in general. The region needs this. China needs it. But Hong Kong has to work at ensuring that its preoccupation with reintegration with China does not divert the process of developing formal and informal strategic regional networks and connections so that it remains an active and important player in the region-wide process of Asianisation. This is not just for Hong Kong itself but for other players in the region, who in return will work hard for Hong Kong's continued participation as a leading city-state or region in the East Asian Community.

If the basic building blocks of this Community could be both nation-states and city-regions, Hong Kong could have a role as an independent player, without threatening the sovereignty over Hong Kong of the Chinese state (any more than it is threatened by other forces in the contemporary world). This is already implicit in the arrangements agreed to by the Chinese Government for Hong Kong's participation in APEC. There is no reason why this could not be applied in other Asian regional arrangements, or why variations on this might not be developed for the free association of all the sub-regions and city-regions in East Asia.

I don't see this as being against China's interests. Indeed, China should welcome this role for Hong Kong. Hong Kong is always spoken of as being useful to China and this is mostly assumed to be commercial and financial, and through its great transport and communication facilities. But Hong Kong has also been critical to China in the period since the Open Door in providing the software of modernisation, for economic management and the opening and restructuring of the Chinese economy. And perhaps most importantly, Hong Kong understands regional nervousness about China, understands the attitudes of others in East Asia and the uses of being a good regional citizen. It has the potential to impart that to China. And it has the potential to be a leading player in a formation of Asian sub-regions, through which China itself could demonstrate its own commitment to regional citizenship. If Hong Kong were able to take up the regional role I have suggested, it will not only be good for the rest of the region and China, it will ensure that Hong Kong itself has a future.

The circumstances of Australia and Hong Kong in relation

to China are almost worlds apart. But in relation to what happens in East Asia over the next 25 to 30 years, there is much in common because this is the habitat in which we will both have to find our future. It is one in which China will have, if it chooses, the capacity to impose its views and its will. This is so close to being true already that its realisation is more fact than probability.

The future for Australia between now and 2020 will be in or alongside an Asia joined in a formalised East Asian Community, political in nature if economic in name.

East Asia needs such a Community, somewhat on the lines of Europe, for the peace, prosperity, security and social and cultural harmony of its region, irrespective of what it might also need, separately, to bridge the Pacific and broker economic relations with the United States or what it might need in a multilateral security arrangement across the Pacific. To maintain that something on the lines of Europe is not possible in East Asia is, depending on where it is coming from, cultural arrogance or cultural cringe, and in any event uninformed.

An East Asian Community is necessary because peace and security and prosperity are not assured; because the benevolence of greater powers towards smaller is never assured—their treatment of smaller powers is seldom equitable, and their own behaviour may not be predictable; because the behaviour of Great Powers is not the only threat to a stable future; and because the legacies of history and culture present political and other problems which can only be managed on a shared basis.

The process of Asianisation now also makes it necessary—necessary to go forward as there is no sanity in trying to go back. East Asian societies are now in such intimate propinquity that they are compelled to understand what this means, find what identity this East Asia has and work out how it can live with itself. It has to be political and cultural. A Community based simply on economic concerns will not suffice. It must be driven by a long-term vision. The model, and some of the conceptual foundations and institutional and consultative processes, already exist in ASEAN and its attendant relationships.

Many things distinguish this ASEAN model from APEC, but two are fundamental. One is that its dynamic is internal, coming from within a core group of Asian nations. The other is that it has its origins in goals of 'solidarity, co-operation and peace', and this is what drives it and determines its character. While the inclusion of, first, security, and, then the environment and human rights on ASEAN's agenda was late in coming, there is a natural fit of these issues to the broad political agenda of ASEAN's Treaty of Amity and Cooperation, notwithstanding that much of what ASEAN is seen to be about is economic. ASEAN is also relatively compact. It has, of course, great internal tensions, but if you are in the business of forging a community of real intimacy between nations of great diversity and rivalry, you are going to have tension. That ASEAN has both produced and managed such tensions indicates its strength and viability. It is not surprising that it was around ASEAN that East Asia coalesced to meet with Europe in March 1996.

There is also a supporting fabric for an Asian Community in East Asia, in the vast and diverse pattern of literally hundreds of multilateral organisations, institutions and associations under various 'Asia' titles, which are explicitly about regional cooperation and which link the region in various configurations and memberships. These range from the governmental, through business and education and the media to non-government organisations. This intertwining has been reflected for some years in the flows of people within the region. Not a day passes without some important meeting on some aspect of regional cooperation. So intensive is this activity that it has created a breed of travelling Asiacrats, who are setting agendas, forcing ideas, making policy.

What will define this Community? With the facilitation of ASEAN, the obstacles and differences are potentially one step down the path to harmonisation. There is no common race. But neither is there shared language, or common culture, or shared history, or common religion, or common philosophy or politics or music or architecture or cuisine. But there is now a common aspiration which is driving the region forward and which will move from a coalition for ASEM purposes to a coalition for an East Asian Community.

The membership of this Community will include all the Asian participants in ASEM, with one or two additions. It will almost certainly be defining and exclusive, and membership will perhaps be fixed and then closed for a set time at the point of its inauguration. It will not include the United States. There will be a charter or treaty, and future membership will be by accession to that. Its terms may be devised to present some difficulty to some of the countries which may wish to accede. Just as ASEAN is now a 'power' in East Asia, so will this

Community be a 'power' in world politics. The projection of China's influence in this can be scaled up or down according to one's preferred analysis. China does not have to be as overwhelmingly predominant as I have suggested, but it will be the dominant power regionally and within any East Asia Community. There are now influential voices in China which see this future and which are seeking to explore terms on which China should start serious engagement with its East Asian partners to put a structure on what has already emerged informally.

Australia may be in this Community. It may not. But it cannot simply go somewhere else. So, whether in or out, it has to live with it.

The handling of this situation will require the most enormous range of skills, and intellect, and knowledge, and vision, and long-term scenarios and planning, and cultural understanding and capacity for two-way communication. And certainty about who we are and what we want to hold onto.

CHAPTER 10

Can Australian society survive?

There may not be an East Asia Community. There does not have to be for Australia to be faced with the dilemma of how to live with this 'power' or region as a cultural and political minority. The question is whether the strengths and attractions of our society will actually be able to survive enough in that future environment to enable us to pursue our kind of dreams.

There are many challenges, but I believe the following are fundamental: what is non-negotiable? do we have the people who can manage our future? are our personal values and relationships in the region strong enough? and can we handle a dominant and totally different political culture? For each of these challenges we must have a strategy to ensure we will still be around in 2020.

WHAT IS NON-NEGOTIABLE?

Every Australian involved in or with the region has an obligation to think deeply about what the engagement with Asia will mean for our society in 30 years' time, and what we as individuals or corporations or governments ought to do. We can see from the example of Europe, where the differences of culture and values are much narrower, what agonies can be presented

159

by the subordination of aspects of national identity to a wider regional identity.

This is also where the debate on the Australian identity and the Republic has to lead us. Some people say the Australian preoccupation with identity is a diversion from the main game, an obsession which a mature and sophisticated society ought to put aside. But the debate on identity has to go deeper, to the ideas and the values and the cultural and philosophical and moral and ethical norms which are fundamental to our society. We *have* to think about what is non-negotiable because already every day we are making decisions which involve choice, and compromise. Many corporations unthinkingly practise a 'when in Rome' policy in Asia. Is there a point where the corporation itself is compromised? What if this compromises some national objective? What if it crosses some principled government policy or national interest? What if many individuals and corporations are in this position? What if governments are themselves making compromises in this way? I am not referring here to compromise under pressure, but compromise simply by witting or unwitting choice in the day-to-day business of dealing with Asia. Nor am I suggesting that compromises are made because Asian societies are by definition unethical or crooked. But if they are different and we are in close relations with them, there are always choices to be made. What I am suggesting is that we already make these choices on small matters or in isolation, and that we are often backing unconsciously towards and perhaps over a line of principle which ought never to be crossed. I believe, for example, that the government compromised its immigration policy when it accepted for permanent residence almost all Chinese students who were in Australia at the time of 4 June 1989. I believe many universities have been compromised in their student recruitment in Asia. The government is compromised by its semantic ducking and weaving over the Dalai Lama. Our ethical beliefs are compromised daily by their selective application in Asia. I know many corporations which are already compromised by acceding to practices which are unethical not only by the judgment of our society but by the judgment of societies in Asia in which they are operating.

If we have not thought about what is non-negotiable, how do we know if we have crossed a line where we have compromised something really important for our society? We have always faced these choices, but where they have been in relation to countries of similar background we have known what the rules are and where lines are crossed, because we don't have to think about them, and the penalties and sanctions are known even if we don't think about the values behind them. But when the other culture is unknown to us, we don't know what is good or bad in its terms, or ethical or unethical. And if we haven't worked out our non-negotiables we don't even know where accommodation ends and compromise begins. Seminars conducted by the St James Ethics Centre and the Asia–Australia Institute reveal that this problem is already with us. If to this situation there is added direct pressure from outside interests or governments it is a very serious matter. We already experience this kind of pressure, and where it is blatant it is often easier to resist. But if we are compromised in other ways we will not always find resistance possible.

We therefore need a public, national process to debate and determine what is non-negotiable for our society, and perhaps we even need something like a bill or charter to affirm it. This is not a matter of a committee drawing up a code of political rectitude; still less is it a matter of preaching to other countries on how they ought to behave on human rights. It is a matter of individuals and corporations and government agencies thinking about what it means, for our democracy, to live in a world dominated by a different and often conflicting set of cultures and values, and setting out to find common ground across Australia and in some form that will be meaningful to most Australians. Perhaps the strongest argument for the Australian republic is that it would provide the occasion for the incorporation of a statement on this matter into the republican charter, and the opportunity in that charter to commit ourselves to *our* values—in the way Asian societies are talking about their values: our values, which may in fact partake of much that is Asian and which for us are the way we want our society to continue to be.

The need for conscious articulation of our values and what is non-negotiable, both *within* our society and for our dealings with East Asia, was illustrated in an extraordinarily dramatic way in the race 'debate' which exploded in Australia in the second half of 1996. The trigger was a statement in the national Parliament of ignorance, bigotry and loathing by an independent MP, Pauline Hanson. This was not the only time Australia has heard such sentiments, and it will not be the last. But what happened on this occasion was that it went almost unchallenged by Australia's political leadership, and by Prime

Minister John Howard, for nearly two months. If we had had some conscious national consensus on the non-negotiables this could not have happened. But political leaders played with the future of Australia, thinking to please a variety of constituencies—people who agreed with all or part of what Ms Hanson had said, people who opposed immigration, Asians, Aborigines, people who felt they wanted a say and had not been allowed to have it. This was an extraordinary way to lead Australia on such an issue—second-guessing the voter.

The Prime Minister at first refused even to comment. When he was finally pulled from his silence by a persistent and ghoulish media, his statements were qualified, diluted and even negated by sentiments to the effect that Ms Hanson was reflecting the attitudes and feelings of Australians, that she 'should be allowed to say' what she had said. The message this sent to Australia and Asia was that the Prime Minister felt he had to condemn what was going on. But the received message both by racists and concerned liberals was 'we all know what he really thinks, don't we'. When it came to his comments on a talk-back radio program on 24 October, the message was: 'I sympathise fundamentally with Australians who are insulted when they are told that we have a racist, bigoted past', 'to tell children who themselves have been no part of it, that we're all part of a sort of racist, bigoted history is something that Australians reject'.[38]

There is a history, and this is the history of where the Prime Minister's words carry conviction. There was conviction in John Howard's statement questioning Asian immigration in 1988; but there was equivocation in his subsequent purported repudiations of this statement. Since becoming Prime Minister in March 1996, his repeated statements that Asia is the focus of his foreign policy come across as without conviction, but his declarations that we are 'not Asian' or 'not part of Asia' carry total conviction, as do his statements about the importance of relations with the United States.[39] His comments against the tide of racist statements in late 1996 carried little conviction for many Australians and for many Asians.

What finally forced the issue was a rash of critical commentary in the East Asian media, from Jakarta to Beijing. Sadly, it was considerations of trade and tourism which seemed to drive the Australian leadership into a resolution passed in the national Parliament. Moral offence which had been quietly building for two months had not been enough. The resolution, dated 30 October 1996, is so important that it is worth quoting:

This House:

Reaffirms its commitment to the right of all Australians to enjoy equal rights and be treated with equal respect regardless of race, colour, creed or origin;

Reaffirms its commitment to maintaining an immigration policy wholly non-discriminatory on grounds of race, colour, creed or origin;

Reaffirms its commitment to the process of reconciliation with Aboriginal and Torres Strait Islander people in the context of redressing their profound social and economic disadvantage;

Reaffirms its commitment to maintaining Australia as a culturally diverse, tolerant and open society united by an overriding commitment to our nation and its democratic institutions and values; and

Denounces racial intolerance in any form as incompatible with the kind of society we are and want to be.

This was cause for celebration, but it is unfortunately not enough. Does the nation support it? Beginning with Bob Hawke, there has been insufficient attempt to debate these issues in a reasoned way and to build a solid national consensus on what is non-negotiable. The task ahead is immense. The damage that was done to our society has to be repaired. The idea that the unspeakable can now be spoken openly, which the failure in leadership encouraged, must be firmly dealt with. But above all, the process of working out what we, all Australians, stand for has to be taken up and pursued until we have something on which most Australians can sign off.

And in Asia? Asians will not easily be persuaded by a latter-day diplomatic offensive that what they perceive to be the reality is mere illusion. It is not a backbench MP they perceive. They have noted the equivocation in the Howard Government's position on Asia, Asian immigration and race, and many remain unconvinced. Australian Government spokespeople seized on a statement by Malaysian Prime Minister Dr Mahathir that this 'debate' would not affect bilateral relations and that Australia is not racist. They failed to recall his earlier private but well-known reflection that John Howard's confident assertion in Jakarta that we are not part of Asia was only what he (Dr Mahathir) had been saying all along. John Howard himself says Asians are not concerned because he had been to Japan and Indonesia and they did not raise it with him. Perhaps one day he will learn how to read, or at least how to find out, how people in Asia think and how they communicate what they think.

The irony is that the leadership's action on this episode, when it did finally act, is a timely illustration of the problem of the challenge we face from Asia. The implied threat to our economic relations drew an almost panicked reaction from the government, a reaction which in this case produced a result which is positive for domestic Australia and the assertion of Australian values. What will we do when that implied threat requires some compromise of Australian values—or when the threat is not implied?

If we think the challenge to our society is overstated, the following may be an indication of what could be. In China's differences with Hong Kong in the last years of British rule, there was a linguistic mismatch reflecting profound differences in political philosophy. China may be more open than it was when Mao died in 1976, but what we witnessed in the exchanges between the Chinese and Hong Kong's British government was China seeking to determine the very definition of the concepts, within which definition the forms and the processes themselves were to be defined and words would have meaning—words like 'free' and 'open' and 'democratic' and 'human rights'. One of the great achievements in the creation of the European Union was that of finding a shared, commonly accepted political language. This meant that common ground could be solid ground. A common political language is what expresses a small 'c' community, and gives it something of the character of a single polity, and a kind of broad, cross-national 'social contract'.

There is nothing like this across Asia yet. There is movement, but the common language still eludes us. We may have common language on trade liberalisation, but when it comes to democracy, humanism, freedom, pluralism, we do not. The Human Rights conference of Asian countries in Bangkok in 1993 illustrated both the forward movement and the distance still to travel. And this distance is part of the reason why Asian countries continue to play with APEC, while waiting for the main event in Asia. This main event waits mainly on two players: on Japan, for it to make up its mind about when it wants to throw in its lot with Asia, and on what common understanding; and on China, for it to decide what kind of power relationships it will accept for itself in Asia, and on what definitions.

Many people in the region have already begun to defer to China, to find open and vigorous discussion of matters unpalatable to the Chinese Government difficult, and to suggest that there is a right way to deal with China, different from the way you deal with anyone else, which means playing on China's rules and definitions. I understand the need for cultural and political sensitivity, but it is hard to see that this deference can be healthy for the future of Asia.

Hong Kong of course is a special case. I know China has conflicts elsewhere in which it has seemed prepared to compromise. But the dispute with Hong Kong has been the one context in which we have been able to observe sustained, concentrated and clearly strongly felt discussion by the Chinese Government on matters which touch so directly on these fundamental issues of openness, diversity and pluralism, the nature of community and polity, equality, and the terms and definitions on which a Chinese government finds relations with others acceptable.

China's management of its economic transition to a freer economy has been masterly. It has shown previously unimaginable flexibility in many areas. Its post-Mao adaptation has carried it into interaction with international society of a kind which most people in China in the 1970s would have thought beyond rational contemplation. And the change will continue on all of these fronts. But on the question of how China will want to run its relations with its neighbours there is also the China of 'political correctness'. As with political correctness in Western countries, this concerns itself with prescriptive practices on what language one may or may not use, how words are defined, the terms in which any issue must be discussed, and the right interpretation of history, democracy and human rights, and other people's motivations. This is not totally unrelieved, but while doctrinaire Maoism has gone, China is still a country in which special terms are reserved for measuring foreigners' behaviour on a scale of political correctness. Official China can still find it possible, for example, to divide foreigners into 'friends of China', 'enemies of China' and people who are 'unreliable' or 'insufficiently friendly', the last usually referring to people who have thought it constructive to be critical.

As we know from the experience of other Great Powers with a strong sense of their destiny in world affairs, political correctness and its extension to other nations under their influence has not been uncommon. There is nothing in history which determines that China will behave in this way, but nor is there

anything which says that it will not. The private view of most
of those I talk to in Northeast and Southeast Asia is that at
this stage the signs are not encouraging. In Australia, we have
to know where we stand.

PEOPLE

The second of the four strategies for our survival relates to the
people we hire today. How does one select and skill people for
managing in a dominant habitat whose most basic terms of
human reference one does not know? It is difficult for many
Australians to understand what this means. Aboriginal Australians would. So would many Asian Australians. But those who
come from the dominant culture in Australia will have to
understand that our future will be like that of Mexicans in
respect of the United States, but with perhaps even greater
culture difference. Or like what people in Taiwan had with the
United States, or post-independence Singaporeans or Malaysians
had with Britain. Or like indigenous Australians have still with
non-indigenous Australia.

So what I am arguing is that what might have been brushed
aside as an option, or 'for some people in the department', or
'for someone else but not me', will become a necessity for all
who aspire to executive or management office and hence for all
who are recruited into positions with that career potential, and
hence also for most people in government and business. We now
need, for the next stage in our history, a workforce which can
give us the capability to move easily and comfortably within
other Asian cultures, here and in Asia, as much at ease as those
who belong to that culture and language, and equally able to
access its information, people, corporations, government and
market. You may say this is impossible save for the select few.
But it is precisely what tens of thousands of Asians are doing
every day, in North America and Australia and Europe, and in
their own and in other Asian countries. And they do it because
they are serious about survival. We have to become successful
chameleons, in the positive sense of that image, or, like the
Greek god Proteus, protean—capable of changing form to adapt
and survive in the locality, without compromising our Australianness or the values and ethical codes we live by.

And it is not something to be left for the day we get around
to it after China is already calling the shots in Asia or on the

eve of the 2020s, because, for the managers and executives of the 2020s, along the way they will find themselves working in an Asian milieu. Staff recruitment and development now have to plan for the needs then, to ensure that these people have or are given the skills to enable them to work proficiently, and competitively, within the context of dominant Asian societies and cultures.

And where competition is involved, the competition for most people will not be—is not now—other Australians. It will not even be other Westerners or 'international'. If we think the English language rules, in the Chinese world across Asia, for every transaction conducted in English there must be a thousand in Chinese. The competition in Asia is Asian. So is the bureaucracy. So is the market.

So also will be the mainstream. I must have talked from one perspective or another about this question of Asia education and skills to a few hundred audiences over the years, and I'm sure most people have sat there thinking—if they didn't disagree—well, yes, but not for me. And for the most part they could feel they were right in terms of the contemporary conventional wisdom. Asia was at the periphery, and skilling for Asia regarded accordingly. But when the mainstream is Asia, the skills and capabilities of the mainstream have to be appropriate for Asia, and for many parts of Asia, and when these *are* mainstream, the dilemma of choosing between skills for one or for another country will not be an acceptable pretext for inaction but must be answered by spreading different country skills across the range of people in an organisation, or by multi-skilling as is common in Europe or Asia. Setting up with one expert will be setting up for non-performance.

The skills for performance in a dominant Asian habitat therefore have to be integral to staff development policies and programs. If we think we can farm them in for a particular job, we will never have managers of our own who can manage effectively in this future habitat. And while we must dramatically expand the use of Asian Australians, this also cannot be allowed to become a pretext for non-Asian Australians simply to opt out.

The most successful Asian countries have recognised the importance of long-term professional development, education and training, in a society dominated by a country with a different culture. The office buildings of Taiwan and South Korea, for example, are littered with graduates from American colleges and universities. You could say that if we wanted to be as successful as the successful Asian countries, our office buildings would be littered with Australians who are graduates from universities in Japan, for example, or Indonesia or China. Maybe, even, 50 per cent of the Australian Cabinet would have PhDs from Asian universities.

There is no program in an Australian corporation or public sector agency, or university, which will deliver such a result. In part this is because the people responsible don't know what to do. So we now have to become focused and professional in the matter of the people who direct development and training for Asia. This does not mean just throwing money at it. If we are to spend money we should spend it on making ourselves more professional at doing it; we have to appoint personnel or 'human resource' managers who are themselves skilled in these fields, study experience in other countries, look at the research, look at what programs are around, look at the outcomes, talk to people who have been through them or had people go though them. And get someone who knows Australia as well as they know Asia.

As I have suggested throughout this book, the hard part of getting into Asia is the culture. It is still often dismissed as 'soft', but it is hard, and the really hard part is yet to come. There used to be a Cold War joke of sorts which went something like: 'Learn to use chopsticks now! Before it becomes compulsory'! I'm afraid the intended import of that quip—in a different time and context and in a cultural and political way and not (necessarily) military—is now compulsory for Australia.

And the measure of performance in this skill, the skill of handling oneself in an Asian cultural habitat? We do have some, but I can't think of any more testing than the capability of sharing a culture-specific joke in someone else's culture and language. But then, we would need an executive or manager to assess the performance!

I have talked to many Australian executives about what skills and qualifications they would see as necessary for an executive or manager—public or corporate—by the 2020s and between now and then. Few had thought about it before. Most find it difficult to come up with anything different from the profile they would seek in the executive for today. Some add a language, usually as desirable rather than essential. Some mention skills to do with information technology. It is therefore essential that we develop some national sense of what skills and qualifications are needed in the people who will have to guide Australia through this next 25 to 30 years. The fact that we could have got it so wrong in Asia suggests that we have nothing like this at present.

Taking as read the specific requirements of the profession or business and general executive and management requirements as they are understood now as necessary within a society like Australia or for dealing with a country like the United Kingdom or the United States, here are some fundamental skills and qualifications for getting us to the year 2020. The ideal profile is someone who can access East Asia and deal with East Asians at home and abroad to equivalent depth and with equivalent success as the best of East Asians now accessing the United States (and Australia) and dealing with Americans (and Australians). Therefore:

- a sound knowledge of East Asian history, politics and cultures, from study and from experience of living and working in the region;
- fluency in at least two of the languages of East Asia, preferably including Chinese;
- qualifications from a graduate school or professional development institution in East Asia;
- strong personal and professional networks in several East Asian countries;
- skill and qualifications in cross-cultural communication, and proven ability in managing in a cross-cultural workplace, i.e. with a cross-cultural board, or senior executive, management or workforce;
- flexibility in adapting/responding to other people, including to their cultural behaviour, communicative styles, and their approaches to negotiation and conflict resolution;
- ability to maximise potential from a minority situation (e.g. in equity participation, executive teams etc.) and skill in making strategic business alliances to preserve independence and flexibility;
- strong self-knowledge in terms of values and ethical beliefs;
- intellectual curiosity about other societies;
- outstanding qualities as a human being and commitment

to the central importance of human beings in all under-
takings.

If this seems a tall order, remember that not a few, but
substantial numbers of people in Asia have such profiles in
respect of the West, and some even, now, in respect of other
Asian countries. We can say this is too hard. But then, we could
also go back to lying on the beach.

It is essential also to underline that this ideal is not for the
select few executives but for all. It has to be for those who work
in Australia and not just for those who work in Asia. It is for
the board and government ministers and senior executives and
departmental heads and managers down the line. It has to be
laterally and not just vertically. It is mandatory for the in-house
legal counsel and the corporate company secretary. And it is
mandatory also for the person in charge of human resources (a
situation I have yet to find in any Australian organisation,
public or private).

To come back to the question of Asian Australians. If they
have the skills, including 'Australia-literacy' and 'Australia
skills', we must make every opportunity for them and us to
make the best use of their skills. But this is not the answer to
the national problem. By the 2020s only 7 to 10 per cent of the
population will be of Asian ancestry. The commitment I am
talking about has to be total, because the challenge does not
stop suddenly at a certain level of management or at the door
of the chief executive or the boardroom or the minister's office.
It is total.

And managers have to know what is going on. In my
consulting firm we recently discussed a code of ethics. The term
'conflict of interest' was readily translated into Chinese. Fine,
I might say as manager. Not fine at all. I look at the Chinese,
and while it is from a dictionary, it is unsatisfactory. And my
Chinese colleagues disagree among themselves on what term is
to be used, and in the course of their discussions great problems
emerge in the understanding of the concept. Because there are
not only linguistic difficulties but also social or cultural differences about obligations, 'conflict of interest' is distressingly
elusive.

Similarly, I have sat with colleagues or clients in a hundred
situations where interpreting leads to great misunderstanding
and mismatch of expectations, because the interpreter, not
being Western, is communicating in a way appropriate to his

or her culture, with indirectness, ellipsis and circumlocution, avoidance of conflict, considerations of face and different understanding of Western legal thinking and documentation which produces translation barely recognisable from the original. I have often been told beforehand by the Australian party that they have this great interpreter—'he's terrific'. How would they know?

RELATIONSHIPS

This brings me to the third strategy, which is about the extent and quality of our personal relationships in the region. Relationships are the single most important thing about dealing with people in and from East Asia, for whatever purpose. They are therefore also the most powerful means of advancing or defending our interests.

The working of personal connections is of course a familiar part of Western societies, and the term 'old boy network' expresses the special nature of ingroup connections, originally in British society. But the strength and import of personal connections is infinitely more important in the societies with which we deal in Asia. This is a cultural matter and in many ways at the heart of the cultural problem faced by Australia. An instructive example of the problem was a recent commentary in *Business Review Weekly* about the troubled Australian transport giant TNT. TNT had over the years bought up many small transport operators in Australia which continued to run as separate businesses under its wing. TNT then sought to combine them to get economies of scale and better margins, but 'TNT fell down because the cultures of the businesses were different'.[40] This was in Australia. In the same society. With the same history and culture and traditions and language and education and broad societal norms. And in the same industry. Translated to an Asian society, the cultural difference is multiplied for every one of these factors, with a concomitant exponential increase in the cultural gap. The cultural differences between Asian societies are of course also great. But one characteristic which they almost all have in common and which distinguishes them most from Australian and other English-speaking Western societies is that they are what social scientists describe as collectivist whereas we are individualistic.

There are many complexities to this distinction (there are

also exceptions to it), but the critical difference is the way in which personal relationships and groups have an almost organic function in a collectivist society and are the dominant motivation in almost every human encounter. Research on collectivist societies concludes, for example, that people in such societies are born into family and other ingroups which protect them in exchange for loyalty; identity is based in the social network to which one belongs; harmony is important and direct confrontation is avoided; communication depends greatly on context and what is unspoken; trespassing on group norms leads to shame and loss of face for self and group; the relationship between employer and employee is perceived in moral terms and hiring and promotion takes the employees' ingroup into account; the relationship prevails over the task.[41]

This is indeed a complex field in which the unsuspecting Australian wanders in innocence. How often have I heard Australians proclaim they are close friends and totally accepted by someone in Asia, when on inspection it is clear that they have not been taken into that person's ingroup but befriended within some circumscribed limit. I have referred earlier to the Australian tendency to see agreement where what they have is assent or silence for the sake of not disagreeing openly or directly. This is not theory but insistent fact. The evening before writing these words I am at an official banquet in Sydney for a Chinese delegation. There is much badinage from the Australians. The Chinese respond in kind. But they are actually very unhappy because someone has stuffed up the protocol. 'See how our good Chinese friends don't care about protocol', someone tells me. 'These people don't have a clue about protocol', I hear the Chinese factotum say in Chinese to the delegation leader, 'I am deeply sorry'.

I see the force of the collectivist imperative every day in my working relationships throughout East Asia and even with my Chinese colleagues in my consulting business in my Beijing office and in Sydney. The imperatives are often so strong that they have the compulsion almost of drugs or hypnosis. Even when it is clearly to personal or company detriment, Chinese colleagues will often feel quite unable to refuse the importunities of Chinese missions on disguised holidays in Australia, 'because they are Chinese'. Group loyalty is paramount. Each person has concentric and overlapping groups—from family, birthplace, school and university to workplace, language and dialect group, social or sporting groups, and business. The group determines not only loyalties but also norms of behaviour; you can for example be dishonest with people who are not part of your ingroup simply because they are not.

There is also no such thing as a front door. People responding to these cultural imperatives will always seek a back-door connection, and go to extreme lengths to avoid dealing with someone they do not know. This is particularly strong in China, where Chinese officials will refuse to supply public information because 'we don't know you'. Professor Wang Gungwu, when vice-chancellor of the University of Hong Kong, related that successions of visitors to his university from the PRC to investigate how to run a modern university would exclaim: 'But how can you do it without bringing in your own people to fill the key positions!'

Australians now have to understand that by definition they are outsiders in Asia. They may get close. They may often think they are closer than they are. But they will never be truly part of the ingroup they are dealing with or courting or aspire to belong to unless they are able to enter into the fullest possible two-way communication.

And this is why, for the Australian future, it is not good enough to leave it to Asian Australians, because this will leave 90 per cent of Australia, of the corporation or the government agency or the university or media organisation—or the Parliament—as outsiders. The effort is for everyone, otherwise we will have repeated experiences like our symbolic exclusion from ASEM.

Is it possible to bridge this gap? It is, and there is only one answer. We have to set out to get inside the Asia ingroup by getting inside the thousands of ingroups with which we deal in Asia every day. This is for us a national necessity. It is also a strategy for survival in a world in which we have no protector. Because we start from the disadvantage of a minority, we have to set out to know more people, more closely, at more senior level, in more countries, than any other nation in the region. And in their language and culture. Where we do not yet have the language we must start with the culture, and where we do not have that we must start with the self-knowledge that we are outsiders and have to find some way of getting onto the inside.

There is unfortunately no institution in Australia with a strategy which could deliver this outcome. But if we can develop this capability, there can be a strategy, and we have a chance. Most Asian societies do not yet know each other well. Their mutual networks are developing fast, particularly within ASEAN, but the ingroups still remain apart. Relations between Singapore and Indonesia provide an example. So there is a chance for Australia. If we can be the best networked country in the whole region, and become accepted as part at least of some ingroups, we can use these connections to secure partici- pation and a voice and a vote in the councils which will decide the region's and our future. This will not happen by us marching up to the front door, or by nation-state positioning and postur- ing, or through such regional structures as APEC or the ARF.

The challenge demands of us not just language and literacy, but great dexterity, without government pushing or forcing, to massage and manoeuvre and manipulate our connections to procure outcomes which ensure not only regional participation for Australia but regional collective commitment to the main- tenance of regional pluralism.

HUMANISM AND THE STRATEGY OF BEING AN EXEMPLAR

The fourth strategy begins with political culture. Throughout this book I have referred to the fact that the difficult and sensitive and intractable problems have to do not with econom- ics but with politics and culture. The United States hounds the PRC on intellectual property; it did nothing about Taiwan when the latter was the world's leading book pirate. This is political, and people in the PRC see it as political. The current internal situation in Indonesia is unstable because it is good economics, but bad politics. The axing of the Development Import Finance Facility (DIFF) by the Coalition Government in 1996 was fis- cally rational, politically mad.

Politics is about people and people issues. Not parties or the political process, but what motivates people, why they have different perspectives on the same thing, how they care about other people and how they act on that. It is also about the issues of the day but not just, for example, the environment, human rights, immigrant labour, rich versus poor, urbanisation, but how these impact on people. Australians probably pride themselves on getting these issues pretty right in Asia, but getting them right in the future is going to be increasingly complex. Why? We used to lecture and hector and preach to others. That was an inappropriate approach in the past, but it is also a two-edged sword. If we establish that the rule in East Asia is to tell others how to run their societies, we will have that turned against Australia. We have to survive by example and exert influence 'by our works'.

These are strategies we ought to be thinking about now for our 30-year future. But Australia doesn't have a 30-year plan, or even a 30-year vision. Having a 30-year vision does not, of course, mean that you can be certain that is how it is going to turn out, but it does mean you know where you hope to end up, that you can set out to try to make as much of that happen as possible, and anticipate developments which threaten your society and move to head them off. Within every one of our institutions, from the Cabinet to the corporation, it has to become an institutional habit of mind to think about the nature of our environment well into the future. Some time ago some people in Japan tried to develop 100-year scenarios, on the argument that if you force yourself to think that far into the future it helps you to think more constructively about 50 years hence, and gives a sharper edge to your thinking about 20 or 30-year plans. In any event, you can't sensibly undertake a 25-year plan unless you have the institutional capacity to project forward and imagine what the world might be like at that time.

The detail, of course, depends on whether you are in politics or government or business or the universities or elsewhere. But in terms of the national interest, long-term thinking must be asking fundamental questions about who should be our closest friends, whose company we are seen to keep, who we go to bat for, who we turn to first when crises loom. It should question the wisdom of being closely aligned with the United States, or other Western powers, or with Japan or China. It should be asking who are our natural friends and allies in Asia, and how we can enter into their ingroups in a way which will ensure the preservation of our particular form of free, open, liberal, humanist and democratic society.

If we do not answer or even ask these questions, the engagement with Asia, instead of being the culmination of an exciting process of change, will end in disappointment, frustration, the erosion of the good life and the possible alienation of the values which make this the society we enjoy so much.

Here is another dilemma. It was economic concerns which finally drove us to discover Asia, but the pre-eminence we give to economic relations with Asia now obscures the political and diminishes the human, yet it is the human which is so much part of what we stand for. The answer for Australia is to find a way back to our essential humanism and to reject the tyranny of economism, for us and I hope also for the region.

In the region, whatever we are engaged in, we should start with the concerns of the human being and give this central and prior importance. This is not about human rights as such, but it may mean that we make different decisions, do things differently or over different time-scales, or walk away from some things—quietly and without self-trumpeting or self-righteousness, but in a way that is considered, principled and consistent. We cannot be absolute or we will have nothing. It is unintelligent and foolish, for example, to be so extreme in the position we take on Myanmar. There are concerned and liberal people in Southeast Asia who believe there are other ways of principled behaviour possible in Myanmar without shouting instructions at the SLORC.

By quietly putting the human being first, we will get the Australian image in Asia right, we will get closer to being inside the ingroups, we will have credit with most governments in the region, we will have good business, and we will establish credentials for an accepted role in the region, as participant, and as helpful and thereby also potentially equal and influential. To be exemplary in this is a way of showing leadership.

VISION

The strategies suggested above are to ensure that we will still be around to enjoy the 2020s. But it is critical also that we have a vision, and know what it is we are working for. We need a vision for ourselves in the region, and a vision for our own society.

The vision I would urge for ourselves and the region is for a political association of East Asian nations suggested at the beginning and throughout this book, in which the countries of Northeast and Southeast Asia are joined as sovereign and equal partners. Sovereignty and equality are critical. So also is philosophy. This community needs to be founded on commitment to an idea of a regional polity which is not only politically and culturally pluralist and non-discriminatory, but humane; which impels its members to harmonious solution of intra-regional problems; which in public policy, particularly in economic planning and the development programs of government and business, gives precedence to the individual and the family; which supports the constituent countries in the development of societies which give centrality to the human being, drawing on both Asian collectivist and Western individualist traditions; and which encourages the growth of educational institutions which provide leadership in these matters through free and open inquiry.[42]

This is achievable. An East Asian Community may already be in formation, but even if it is not it is in any event necessary, for the peace and stability of the region and for the region to be capable of resisting the hegemonism of any one culture or the homogenisation of all. It is only within such a community that Australia has a chance of retaining its independence and ensuring the preservation of its humanism and its democracy and offering leadership in this way.

Many in Asia would question this role for Australia. I accept that there are many paradoxes in our past and our present. But if we can do most of the things suggested in this book we can be a quiet exemplar. Recognition of this is already implicit in the attitudes of those in Asia who criticise Australia for its failings but turn to it when circumstances force permanent departure from their own countries, or for the education of their children, or for a back-up base for their business or for security in retirement. They do not articulate the reasons, but they all have to do with the strong democratic traditions of our society.

Australia no longer has a White Australia policy, which is not to say that bigotry and racism have been expunged from the breast of every Australian. But White Australia has been officially dead for nearly two decades, and from where Australia started out, that is an achievement. Australia is tolerant in its domestic life. The same easygoing nature of Australia made us lazy about acculturation to our neighbours, but the tolerance of Australians has an important outcome in the openness and stability of our democratic society. We have had a shocking record towards the Australian indigenous people, our institutions are flawed, and the principles by which we live are marred by human error, misdemeanour and failure. But in general our citizens live their lives relatively free from coercion or over-much regulation. Our openness and tolerance have the *potential* to make us not only the most interesting and attractive society in Asia but also one of the most dynamic. We have tolerance, ease of movement, and social mobility. We have a pluralist political system, and institutions and underlying values which are informed by humanism and founded also in science and reason.

Australia not only has openness and tolerance, it has a great sense of humour and a capacity to laugh at itself. We also happen to have at least amicable relations with every country in Asia, and with most in the world for that matter. When you look around the world today this is not always common, and it has a positive value for anyone living and working here.

A vision for Australia in the 2020s, which is not yet the Australia of the present but which starts from what we have now, would draw from history, and the example of small states where commerce and the arts and people came together and mingled in an open and supporting polity, and produced enormous creative energy, economic wealth, and cultural originality—the city-states of the European Renaissance, which are one model (albeit one which stamps us culturally), but others, such as the capital of Tang Dynasty China. There have been in history, in different parts of the world, cases of such small societies open to people from outside and welcoming to political and intellectual and economic refugees, and open domestically to talent and ideas, which have become havens for people of talent, and have nurtured that talent into major creativity and great contribution to the advancement of civilisation. They have been trading societies, and they also have been societies in which many foreign languages have been spoken. We have the elements of such a society in embryo.

What we are talking about for the future of Asia in our education is not matched in the education systems in any other country in the region. Our willing and non-discriminatory acceptance of people from other parts of the region for permanent settlement is making for a dynamic mix of a kind which has never before existed in Australia, and is nowhere else in Asia. This will help make Australia a more sophisticated and cosmopolitan society. And it will change the complexion of Australians, literally. Already the cities of Melbourne and Sydney have taken on a different hue. Australia is already the most outward-looking of all the countries of the region, and potentially the most 'Asian'. It does not wish to dominate the region. It is also the one society in which there is no constraint on intellectual freedom or the discussion of the difficult issues which will confront the countries of the region as they wrestle with the problems of closer association. I am not one to project Australia in self-aggrandisement. But Australia could make for itself an opportunity for a brokering role, if it can be modest and not claim this role, proclaim it, or crow about success. But if it can become an intelligent and excellent country, this role is possible.

My concern about Australia's performance in the past is balanced by my belief that this can be Australia's future: the lazy country can be a lovely country and the white society can be a honey-coloured society. The prospects for Australia are exciting beyond imagination.

In political freedom and effective democracy, in contemporary cultural creativity and productivity, in the diversity of a multiculture, in ease of social relations between different income and ethnic groups, in inventiveness and originality, in economic opportunity, in lifestyle—and in everything that is open, cosmopolitan, liberal and humane, this honey-coloured society has a possible future as *the* most attractive society in the world.

But this will not just happen. To get there we have to wrestle with the two sides of our character. We have to start to be intelligent, intellectual, forward-thinking and long-term, and not lazy, about ourselves, our values, our institutions, or our region. We have to take up on our own what is really hard about this, and not clutch at protectors or a white man's world now gone or a past which cannot be retrieved. We have to be a nation of bilingualists, of cultural proteans, literate in Asia and in much else besides. We have to face hard choices and make hard decisions about education and ethics and the economism which eats at our humanism. We have to be Australian and not European, we have to be quiet not strident, we have to learn humility, and to listen to silence. We have to care intensely about the future and the survival of this democracy, one of the oldest in the world, and the preservation of the innate democratic instinct of its people.

We have to find our pilgrim soul.

Endnotes

1 'East Asia' means the countries of Northeast Asia (China, including Taiwan, Hong Kong and Macao, Japan, South and North Korea, and Mongolia) and Southeast Asia (Brunei, Indonesia, Malaysia, the Philippines, Singapore, Thailand, Vietnam, Cambodia, Laos and Myanmar). The ASEM meeting had no representation from Mongolia, North Korea, Cambodia, Laos or Myanmar. My own definition of 'East Asia' would include Australia, and New Zealand if it wishes, and perhaps Pacific Russia, but not Russia as a whole.

2 Gareth Evans, 'Australia in East Asia and the Asia-Pacific: Beyond the Looking Glass', No. 14 in the series The Asia Lectures, the Asia–Australia Institute, Sydney, 20 March 1995.

3 Asian Studies Council, *A National Strategy for the Study of Asia in Australia*, Canberra: AGPS, 1988.

4 See, for example, his comments on Radio Australia, 18 September 1996.

5 Council of Australian Governments, *Communiqué*, Hobart, February 1994.

6 Nancy Viviani (ed.), *The Abolition of the White Australia Policy: The Immigration Reform Movement Revisited*, Centre for Study of Australia–Asia Relations, Griffith University, 1992.

7 Second-generation in-group marriage refers to Australian-born brides and grooms with mother born in country of origin marrying grooms and brides themselves born in, or with one or both parents born in, the same country of origin. Charles A. Price, 'Ethnic Intermixture in Australia', *People and Place*, Australian Forum for

Population Studies, Monash University, Melbourne, vol. 1, no. 1, 1993.

8 Anne Kent, 'Australia in China 1991–1995', in *Australia in World Affairs 1991–1995*, London: Oxford University Press, forthcoming 1997.

9 'Australia and Its Neighbours: An Educational Aspect'. Oration to the Australian College of Education, Fifth National Conference, 1964.

10 *The Teaching of Asian Languages and Cultures in Australia*. Report of the Commonwealth Advisory Council (the Auchmuty Report), Commonwealth of Australia, 1970.

11 *Alfonso Japanese* (for Australian high school students), Melbourne: Curriculum Corporation, 1990.

12 Asian Studies Association of Australia, *Asia in Australian Education*, Sydney, 1980.

13 Asian Studies Council, *A National Strategy for the Study of Asia in Australia*, Canberra: AGPS, 1988.

14 *Immigration. A Commitment to Australia*. Report of the Committee to Advise on Australia's Immigration Policies, Canberra: AGPS, May 1988.

15 *The Humanities in American Life. Report of the Commission on the Humanities*, Berkeley: University of California Press, 1980.

16 Allan Bloom, *The Closing of the American Mind*, New York: Simon & Schuster, 1987.

17 'The Humanities and the Challenge', Australian Academy of the Humanities *Proceedings*, no. 14, p. 128.

18 *Priorities in Higher Education—A Report by the Senate Standing Committee on Employment, Education and Training*, Canberra: AGPS, 1990.

19 *Asia in Australian Higher Education. A Report of the Inquiry into the Teaching of Asian Studies and Languages in Higher Education* (the Ingleson Report), Sydney, University of New South Wales, January 1989.

20 Joseph Lo Bianco, *National Policy on Languages*, Canberra: AGPS, 1987.

21 *Australia's Language, The Australian Language and Literary Policy*, Canberra: AGPS, August 1991.

22 See for example the *Australian*, 3 September 1990.

23 The Australian Education Council, *The Hobart Declaration on Schooling*, Hobart, 1989.

24 See the recommendations of the Rudd Report prepared for COAG, *Asian Languages and Australia's Economic Future*, 1994.

25 W. H. Goodenough, 'Cultural Anthropology and Linguistics', 1957, quoted in J. B. Price (ed.), *Cross-Cultural Encounters*, Melbourne: River Seine Publications, 1985.

26 Currently, Department of Employment, Education, Training and Youth Affairs (DEETYA).

27 See Chapter 5, note 6.
28 *Towards a New Asia. A Report of the Commission for a New Asia*, Kuala Lumpur: Institute for Strategic and International Studies, January 1994.
29 *Perceiving Business Ethics*, Australian–Asian Perceptions Project Working Paper No. 3, Academy of Social Sciences in Australia and the Asia–Australia Institute, University of New South Wales, Sydney, February 1994, p. 6.
30 R. Armstrong, 'An Empirical Investigation of International Marketing Ethics: Problems Encountered by Australian Firms ', *Journal of Business Ethics* 11, 1992, p. 165, cited in *Perceiving Business Ethics*, pp. 4–5.
31 *Perceiving Business Ethics*, pp. 3–4.
32 'Ethical managers make their own rules', *Harvard Business Review*, September–October 1987, p. 69.
33 World Bank, Global Economic Prospects; 'The Global Economic Survey', *Economist*, 1 October 1994; and applying IMF adjustments of traditional GDP for Purchasing Power Parity.
34 *Asian Business Review*, July 1996, p. 12.
35 Shintaro Ishihara, *The Japan That Can Say No*, New York: Simon & Schuster, 1991. See also Shintaro Ishihara and Mahathir Mohamad, *The Voice of Asia*, Tokyo: Kodansha, 1995 (originally published in Japanese as *The Asia That Can Say No*), and *China Can Say No (Zhongguo keyi shuo bu)*, Beijing: Zhonghua Gongshang Lianhe Press, 1996.
36 Richard Hughes, *Borrowed Place, Borrowed Time: Hong Kong with Many Faces*, London: Deutsch, 1976.
37 Formerly professor of Far Eastern History and director of the Research School of Pacific Studies at the Australian National University, and vice-chancellor of the University of Hong Kong until 1965.
38 *Sydney Morning Herald*, 25 October 1996, p. 1.
39 See Richard McGregor in the *Australian*, 30 October 1996, p. 13.
40 Robert Gottliebsen, *Business Review Weekly*, 29 July 1996, p. 6.
41 Geert Hofstede, *Cultures and Organisations: Software of the Mind*, London: McGraw-Hill, 1991, p. 43.
42 This is the vision I have also written into the current vision statement of the Asia–Australia Institute.

Index

TIGERS

Leaders of the new Asia–Pacific

GREG SHERIDAN

Tigers is a unique study of some of the most powerful political leaders in the new Asia, based on scores of exclusive interviews and a decade's work travelling in and reporting on the region. From Taiwan's Lee Teng-hui to America's Bill Clinton, from Singapore's Lee Kuan Yew to the Philippines' Fidel Ramos, from Korea's Kim Young-sam to Malaysia's Dr Mahathir, *Tigers* offers a distinctive interpretation of each leader's career, policies, successes and failures.

Tigers is also the story of the region itself, the dramatic changes in the way its peoples live, and the new patterns of power and authority that have emerged.

Greg Sheridan is the Foreign Editor of the *Australian* and the editor of *Living with Dragons* (1994).

ISBN 1 86448 153 6

LIVING WITH DRAGONS

Australia confronts its Asian destiny

edited by

GREG SHERIDAN

Living with Dragons is a dispatch from the front-line of Australia's engagement with Asia. It reveals for the first time just what a transforming and pervasive development the 'Asianisation' of Australian life is.

Living with Dragons tackles all the hard questions. Australian identity, human rights, economic policy, the environment, defence and security, culture, the business challenge, language and education. Just as the decision a century ago to reject Asia set the pattern for Australia's development, Australia is making the decisions now which will once again determine how we live for the next hundred years. This is the book which tells us what those decisions are, how we have arrived at them and where we go from here as we confront our Asian destiny.

Contributors include Kevin Rudd, Paul Barratt, Tricia Caswell, Michael O'Connor, Gareth Evans, Michael Costello, Linda Jaivin, Stephen FitzGerald, George Yeo, Noordin Sopiee, Michael Easson, Tony Abbott and Mark Ryan.

ISBN 1 86373 880 0

SOUTHEAST ASIA

An illustrated introductory history

6th Edition

MILTON OSBORNE

Students of Southeast Asian history will be grateful to Milton Osborne for writing this appealing and intelligent tour de force—the book is a triumph of organisation.

DAVID P. CHANDLER, *Australian Outlook*

...an introduction that will guide and stimulate beginning students of Southeast Asian history.

M.C. RICKLEFS, *History Today*

Southeast Asia has become the most widely read introduction to the region and this expanded, illustrated edition maintains its reputation as a highly readable survey of the major themes and developments in Southeast Asia's modern history. Extensively illustrated with maps, prints and photographs, it is indispensable reading not only for the student of Southeast Asia but also for the visitor who wishes to gain an insight into its rich and diverse history.

Dr Osborne's clear grasp of his subject reflects his almost continuous association with Southeast Asia for 30 years. He was Director of the British Institute in Southeast Asia from 1975 to 1979 and has taught in Australia, the United States and England as well as publishing several books and a large number of articles on Southeast Asia.

ILLUSTRATED

ISBN 1 86373 823 1

SOUTHEAST ASIA IN THE 1990s

Authoritarianism, democracy and capitalism

edited by

KEVIN HEWISON, RICHARD ROBISON AND GARRY RODAN

Southeast Asia in the 1990s is a book of original case studies about the different political outcomes which flow from industrialisation and economic development. It evaluates the various academic approaches to these questions, and then turns to a series of case studies of Southeast Asian countries. These examine changes to, and tensions in, existing patterns of military rule, authoritarianism, and the progress of democracy as capitalism cuts a swathe through contemporary Southeast Asia.

Southeast Asia in the 1990s provides invaluable, up-to-date and informed analysis of the very rapid political and economic changes taking place in the most dynamic region of the world.

Contributors include Melanie Beresford, Geoffrey Gunn, Harold Crouch and Jane Hutchison.

ILLUSTRATED

ISBN 1 86373 230 6

NEGOTIATING CHINA

Case Studies and Strategies

CAROLYN BLACKMAN

. . . a map, a compass, a signposted path, in accessible, anecdotal and research-backed prose.

STEPHEN FITZGERALD
Chairman, Asia–Australia Institute

. . . a deeply informative primer for dealing with China and the Chinese, rich in anecdotes and revealing in its perceptions . . .

TONY WALKER
China Correspondent, *Financial Times*

. . . an essential read for anyone thinking of doing business in China . . . practical, instructive and above all entertaining. Don't even think of leaving home without it.

BILL O'SHEA
President, Australia–China Chamber of Commerce and Industry

The Chinese have a long tradition of negotiation and use their skills deliberately and effectively. Carolyn Blackman draws on intensive case studies and her clear cultural understanding to reveal the tactics, conscious or unconscious, used by the Chinese, to explain why those tactics are used and to suggest how you might respond to them.

If you're dealing with the Chinese, whether in business, travel or even cultural exchange, *Negotiating China* will put you in a better position to accommodate their concerns and achieve your result.

Carolyn Blackman has been negotiating with the Chinese since 1967 and is currently Director of the Asian Studies Unit, University of Ballarat, and Vice-President of the Australia–China Chamber of Commerce and Industry.

ISBN 1 86448 070 X